C000114564

DEZYDERY CHLAPOWSKI AT THE WRITING OF THE MEMOIRS

To Caroline

THE PUBLISHERS WOULD LIKE TO GIVE SPECIAL THANKS TO
MATT SOBIESZCZYK
AND
TED PAWLOWSKI
FOR THEIR INVALUABLE ASSISTANCE IN PROVIDING MANY
OF THE ILLUSTRATIONS

© Emperor's Press

All rights reserved. No part of this publication may be reproduced, stored in a retrieval system, or transmitted, in any form, or by any means, electronic, mechanical, photocopying, recording, or otherwise, without the prior written permission of the author.

Original Edition; Published in 1992

Printed and Bound in the United States of America

ISBN 0-9626655-3-3

THE EMPEROR'S PRESS
5744 West Irving Park Road
Chicago, IL 60634 U.S.A.
Toll Free, if calling in U.S.A: 1-800-59-EAGLE
Calling from outside U.S.A: 312-777-8864
"Simply the Finest!"

*EXAMPLE OF A VIRTUTI MILITARI
AWARDED TO CHLAPOWSKI*

Memoirs of a
Polish Lancer

The Pamietniki Of
Dezydery Chlapowski

Translated By
Tim Simmons

The Emperor's Press
Chicago, Illinois
"Simply the Finest!"

FOREWORD FROM THE TRANSLATOR

I acquired a copy of Chlapowski's Pamietniki [memoirs] while serving in Warsaw in 1987, but did not read them until my return to London the following year. I was immediately hooked, and spent many a lunchtime enthusing about them to a friend. In an attempt, I suspect, to make me shut up, he suggested I try my hand at a translation. This took me a little over two years. This book is the end result.

THE MEMOIRS

Chlapowski completed his memoirs in 1837. They were in two volumes: the first, which is contained in this translation, covered his experiences during the Napoleonic wars between 1807 and 1813. Chlapowski was in infantry officer at the siege of Danzig in 1807, where he was captured. He served on the Emperor's staff in Spain in 1808 and in the war with Austria the following year. He then joined the Polish Lancers of the Imperial Guard and took part in the invasion of Russia in 1812, and in the early stages of the campaign in Germany in 1813. Chlapowski left Napoleon's service shortly after the battle of Bautzen, after he discovered that the Emperor was prepared to abandon the Polish cause in exchange for peace.

The second volume of the memoirs, which does not appear here, concerns Chlapowski's part in the rebellion against Russia of 1830, in which he held the rank of general.

THE LANGUAGE

Chlapowski's Polish, while occasionally stiff in style, differs little from the language as it is spoken today. The main curiosity is his extensive use of French, which probably reflects three influences: first, French was habitually spoken by Polish gentlemen of his day; second, the Polish armed forces were organized after the French model and used much of its terminology; and finally, of course, Chlapowski himself spent many years at the Court of the French Emperor.

I have stuck as close to the original Polish as possible, but have had to change the odd word or restructure a sentence where the meaning would otherwise have been lost. Place names are given as Chlapowski offers them, sometimes in the Polish, and sometimes in the German or Russian versions. The structure of the memoirs is straightforward, with each chapter covering a specific year. While the story reads for the most part like a diary, Chlapowski occasionally pauses to consider the moral or practical lessons of an incident. These digressions interrupt the flow of the story, but contain some of the most interesting material. See, for example, his reflections on the relative merits of British and French cavalry sabres (in 1808), or his comments on the ideal proportions of Infantry and Cavalry to be combined in an advance guard (in 1813).

THE MEMOIRS AS HISTORY

Like all diarists, Chlapowski should be read with caution. He writes some 20 years after the events he describes and he almost certainly has an axe to grind. But I suggest that this healthy warning need apply more rigorously to a student of purely Polish history than to the reader interested in the wider Napoleonic picture. Chlapowski certainly admired the French Army, but he did not write his memoirs in order to glorify Napoleon or to puff up the reputation of the French military machine. He was a foreigner of junior rank who at the same time had privileged access to the Emperor's Court. As such, he betrays neither the implausible boasting of Marbot, nor the self-justification of Marshal Macdonald. He is able to say that the fighting at Aspern in 1809 convinced him that the French infantry was the best in the world, yet he makes no bones about the rout of Ney's conscripts at Lutzen four years later.

So why did Chlapowski write his memoirs? One factor will no doubt have been that, like many of his contemporaries, he wanted to record his exploits before they were forgotten. He will also have been motivated by a strong sense of Polish patriotism, writing as he did in the aftermath of another failed attempt to reassert Polish independence. The reader will quickly realize that the Polish troops Chlapowski saw on campaign were always the finest and bravest to be found. But perhaps the strongest reason was a desire to clear his own name.

Chlapowski had taken part in the 1830 rebellion against Russia as a general officer, commanding first a flying column, and then, fleetingly, all the Polish forces in Lithuania. He was criticized afterwards for the failure of the Lithuanian expedition, which had ended with the internment of his force by the military authorities of East Prussia. The second volume of Chlapowski's memoirs was an account of these events, in which he attempted to set the record straight, and to prove that defeat had become inevitable before command passed to him. Here was his axe, and it is here that we ought to be most wary of accepting his word.

We need be less cautious about the first, Napoleonic, volume that is printed here, as his ulterior motive in writing this will at worst have been to demonstrate his own good credentials as a soldier and a Pole, and not to misrepresent the activities of Napoleon.

It may seem self-evident to the modern reader that Chlapowski had been an exemplary patriot in his early career, but it would have been less so to some of his contemporaries. The disappearance of an independent Polish State in the last century subjected Polish society to conflicting influences and pressures. Even among those who were committed to regaining independence, there were different interpretations of what action lay in the best interests of the Polish people. For example, there was rivalry and suspicion within the leadership of the 1930 rebellion between those who had served in the army of the Duchy of Warsaw and those who, like Chlapowski, had joined Polish units in French service. The former often felt the latter had put self interest before patriotic duty, while the latter scorned the former as military amateurs. During the Napoleonic wars themselves the rivalry had been largely healthy, and there had in fact been considerable interchange between the two. But the passage of time embittered relations, and in the charged atmosphere after the failure of the 1830 rebellion Chlapowski's past loyalty was brought into question. He is therefore determined, in describing his early career, to underline that he did what he did for Poland. For example, he describes in detail his meeting with Tadeusz Kosciuszko, leader of the 1794 rebellion against Russia and Prussia, and claims at various points that he had the blessing of this famous patriot. Chlapowski is also careful to stress that he left Napoleon's service the moment he discovered, in 1813, that the Emperor was prepared to give Poland up in exchange for peace.

No doubt Chlapowski also wanted, in the first volume, to remind the reader that he had studied the art of war with the greatest military leader of the age. If blame was to be apportioned for the failure of the 1830 rebellion, none should be attached to him!

If the above explanation approaches the truth, it is good news for the reader who is looking for a reasonably unbiased account of Napoleon's campaigns by someone who was at the center of the action. Whatever his motive for writing them, I hope that others will find Chlapowski's memoirs as interesting and challenging as I did.

DEZYDERY CHLAPOWSKI

NAPOLEON AT JENA, 1806 — THE VICTORY THAT GAVE HIM POLAND

THE WAR OF 1807

If only the young had wisdom and the old had strength.

This thought prompts me to write my memoirs: perhaps the young can learn something from them which will make up even a little for their inexperience. For this reason I intend to describe the events which I witnessed, rather than my personal adventures; and to describe only such of these as clarify the wider picture. And so I will not start from my birth and upbringing, but from the events which have general interest and significance.

In November 1806, the French armies arrived in Poznan [Posen].[1] The 1st Chasseurs à Cheval, under Colonel Exelmans, who would later become a famous general, were the first to enter the city as evening fell. The 1st squadron hurried at the trot right through the city with swords drawn, to place pickets on the other side of the river Warta, on the Warsaw and Torun [Thorn] roads. The rest of the regiment stood peacefully in the market square, where a part of the population came cheering to welcome them. I say part because, even by that time, half the population were foreigners. Our ancestors with their customary tolerance had allowed refugees from the religious wars in Germany to settle there, and after the partition of our country many more had come flooding in. After the creation of the Duchy of Warsaw a lot of them left again, especially officials, but in 1806, as today, they made up half of the population of Poznan.[2]

The French squadrons in the market square dismounted, and after talking to the townspeople pressing around them, they confirmed the impression already gained from a few days march through Wielkapolska [West Poland] that they were in friendly territory. They billeted themselves peacefully around the city. General Dabrowski arrived two days later,[3] and finding a number of citizens who had already gathered from the countryside, he formed them straight away into a guard of honor to greet Napoleon. He gave command of this 100 man unit to Uminski, whom he had known from the Kosciuszko war as a 15 year old aide to General Madalinski.

While we waited for the arrival of the Emperor, the Guard of Honor mustered daily in a field, near the river Buk behind the windmills, where it practised platoon and squadron maneuvers. Uminski made me the squadron's adjutant and instructor, for he knew that I had served four years in the dragoons, who at that time served both mounted and on foot. They were a formation armed originally with the "dragon", hence their name, and in Prussia were later turned into light cavalry.

When I had been in Prussian service, I had spent only six weeks a year with the regiment when it went on maneuvers. The rest of the time I had studied in Berlin at the Military School, which at that time was run by artillery and engineer officers, some of whom were to become famous, like Scharnhorst, then a captain and a teacher of mine, later the creator of the national levy [the Landwehr]. My instructor, or rather my co-repetitor, had been Lieutenant Perlitz, with whom I would repeat the lessons taught during the course. I had served from 1801 to 1805. In that last year, when my regiment received the order to march to the Rhine, my father,

---

1 Geographical names are spelt as Chlapowski did, but other common versions will be given as they often appear in maps and histories.

2 Today for Chlapowski was the 1830s.

3 Dabrowski was a veteran of the Kosciuszko insurrection, and was later commander-in-chief of the Polish Legion in Italy. He was recalled to Poland to command the new Polish army prior to the creation of the Duchy of

GENERAL DABROWSKI ARRIVES IN POZNAN

who did not want me to break up my studies, arranged with its commander, General Brusewitz, for my release, and so I stayed in Berlin until the French arrived in 1806.

And so for that reason Uminski used me, perhaps the youngest member of the Guard of Honor, to teach the drill he did not know himself. For although he has been Madalinski's aide, he had never served in a line regiment, and only learned these skills later. Foot drill went very well with such enthusiastic citizens as these, but mounted drill was very difficult as their horses were all too lively for the ranks and kept breaking up the lines.

One should avoid putting over-lively horses in the ranks, as horses always become livelier still when brought together. It is a pleasure to recall that serving in the Guard of Honor were Suchorzewski, Morawski, Tomicki and Ziemecki, all destined to become generals. Also our legionaries[4] arrived one by one from Italy: General Kosinski, Sokolnicki, Downarowicz, Serawski, Machowski, Hanke, Gedrowski, etc, etc. They were warmly welcomed among us.

The arrival of the first French infantry division, belonging to Davout's Corps, made a strange impression on me. A dozen or so of us rode out to meet it, and about a mile outside the city we saw the fields completely covered with individual soldiers, in greatcoats of every color, carrying their muskets with the butts in the air and picking dry paths through the fields to avoid the knee-deep mud on the road.

Right outside the city, by the windmills, there was a beating of drums, and they all came running to form ranks and in the blinking of an eye they had taken off their greatcoats, straightened their bicornes on their heads (at that time the French infantry still wore bicornes) and become the most regular of armies. They then marched at a lively pace into the city with bands playing. They halted in the market square, stacked their weapons and took out little brushes to wipe the mud from their shoes and began fooling around as if they had only been marching for a mile, not the 150 miles they had just completed.

FRENCH SOLDIERS ON THE MARCH

I stared in amazement at these boisterous infantrymen, so far undefeated. They might as well have been going to a dance. They were not like the Prussian infantry from the garrison which had marched out a few weeks before. Those had seemed a full head taller, with broader shoulders and far stronger, but, at the same time stiff and wooden, and after a half-mile march, when their column had halted for some reason, they had straight away broken ranks to rest.

4 Veterans of the Polish Legion provided the cadre for the new Polish army

I knew from military history that it is the infantry that win battles, or rather they are the decisive arm, and if the cavalry sometimes decide the outcome, they usually do so by exploiting the fruits of the infantry's efforts. Studying this gallant and animated French infantry, I understood this truth better, and resolved to serve in the coming war as an infantryman.

The news finally arrived that Napoleon was coming to Poznan. Our Guard of Honor marched out immediately, and was to wait at Miedzyrzecz, in order to greet him at the Polish frontier. But when we were at Bytyn, where we had camped on the way, the Emperor arrived in the night and ordered us to escort him riding before and behind his carriage. He ordered the Chasseurs of the Guard, that is the detail of an officer and 25 troopers who had escorted him thus far, to take up the rear, undoubtedly as a sign of his trust in us.

The night was dark and all I could see was the white turban on the head of the Mamluke Roustam, who was riding postilion on the Emperor's carriage. The Emperor would chat to General Dabrowski through the carriage windows whenever we stopped to change horses, and also a few times on the road, when the deep mud slowed his heavy carriage to a crawl.

When we arrived at the Jesuit mission in Poznan, we were ordered to leave the 25 Chasseurs on duty, and a good room was allocated to us.

The next day at about 10 o'clock, the Emperor mounted his horse and, finding our guard saddled in the courtyard, ordered four of us to ride ahead, and the rest behind him. The Emperor rode across the bridge and onto the Warsaw road, and galloped through the most dreadful mud as far as Swarzedz, where he turned right off the road beyond the village, and set off through the fields in search of high ground. Once there he halted, and gazed at the countryside around him as if he could see an army deployed before him. As I was one of the four horsemen who rode ahead, I had a chance to study him at close hand when we halted. It seemed as if I had known him for a long time, he was so like his portraits, especially those of him on horseback. Yet it was hard to judge the color of his eyes; they were so mobile that I could not study them. At the time they seemed dark, probably because they were so deep-set. But later, when I was able to get closer to him and spoke often with him, I discovered they were very light. When he spoke he would not look into a person's eyes, but would look down or to one side, and only rarely did he look you full in the face.

We returned to the city about five o'clock. The next day he set out on horseback again at about mid-day, and ordered that his route take in a Polish palace. He set off at a gallop on the Sleszew road, and we did not slow down until we reached Kondrzew.

On the third day, 13 December, he ordered us to ride in the opposite direction. We went first to Winiar, where he stopped a few times and looked at the surroundings. Then he set off across the fields, through mud which his horse could hardly wade through. The rest of his escort could no longer follow him, as our four horses, the Emperor's and those of the generals in his entourage stirred up the mud so as to make it impassable.[5]

And so with we four Poles and two French Chasseurs, he rode to Radojew, took the ferry to Owinsk and looked around the deserted monastery there. He asked how such treasures could now belong to the Countess Treskowa. I was able to satisfy his curiosity, as by chance

5 Note in the original Polish edition, presumably written by one of Chlapowski's sons: I draw the reader's attention here to an event during this ride, which had an influence on the author's later service. When at one point, none of the French officers would attempt to cross a muddy ditch into a field, the author leapt the ditch crying "Un Polonais passe partout" (A Pole can go anywhere), and the Emperor followed his example. After the peace of Tilsit the Emperor called for the young Pole "qui passe partout," and made him an ordnance officer.

I knew this family. My aunt, Madame Engestroemowa, who was born a Chlapowska, lived in the Treskow house in Berlin, and I used to dine there every Sunday. In 1804 my aunt showed great civility to Marshal Duroc, who had come in a special deputation to announce the news of the Emperor's coronation, and had everywhere met a chilly reception except in my Aunt's house. For in Berlin at that time, they did not like the French, and were not yet afraid of them. Marshal Duroc remembered my aunt and her kind hospitality, and must certainly have told the Emperor of this, and I suppose that is why, that evening when we returned to Poznan from Owinsk, the Emperor called for me and bade me sit at his table.[6] Besides me, there was only Berthier, Chief of Staff to the whole army, who sat facing the Emperor. The table was so small that only one more person could have sat at the table facing me: only one servant waited on us.

It seemed to me that dinner lasted no longer than half an hour. Yet in the course of that half hour, the Emperor asked me about very many things. He fired questions at me as if I was sitting an exam. He already knew from our conversations on the road that I had served in the Prussian army, so he asked about my studies there, about my artillery instructors, about the organization of the artillery and of the whole Prussian army, and finally he asked how many Poles were likely to be in the Corps which was still in East Prussia beyond the Vistula under General Lestoq. I could not answer this question but pointed out that most of this Corps must be Lithuanians, as it had been mainly recruited in Lithuania. At that time, since the last partition, the whole district of Augustow belonged to Prussia. I also explained that in Lithuania only the gentry were Polish, and the people Lithuanians. He did not know anything about Lithuania, even how it had come to be united with Poland. So he was surprised when I told him that the soldiers serving in the Prussian corps at Krolewiec [Konigsberg] were not Poles but Lithuanians and Samogitians, and that although these spoke little Polish they, like all Russian Lithuania, felt tied by history to Poland. He also asked me about the plight of the peasantry. I knew from my father that the peasantry had been less burdened by serfdom in Polish times. Agriculture had been simpler, and except at harvest had needed fewer hands. But when the Prussian government seized the country, it divided up all the church, royal and common land and gave this to its Germans. These people were very resourceful and increased their demands of the serfs, insisting that the peasants give them more working days and introducing many new forms of service. Our own citizens, crippled with debts from the recent wars, studied the ways of these foreigners and began, at least in part, to follow their example.

The Emperor listened patiently and carefully to all these details. At length he asked about the Jews, who he thought had come to us from Asia. I replied that, on the contrary, they had come to us from the west, when they had been chased out of the rest of Europe, for our ancestors had been tolerant towards all faiths.

He bade me explain how the Principality of Prussia had come into the hands of the Brandenburg Electors (I did not yet know France, so I did not realize how little they are interested by the outside world. They all know the gossip of the French court by heart, but know next to nothing of the history of other countries).

He also asked politely about my parents, and learning that my mother came from Krakow, he asked about that region and the University, about which I knew very little at that time. All I could tell him was where it was, that it had once been very powerful and that there had been

6 Note in the original Polish edition: Gazeta Poznanska of 7 January, 1807 reports that on 13 December, Emperor Napoleon invited to dinner the son of a former comrade of Kosciuszko.

a dispute between the Jesuits and the Academy of Krakow.

After coffee, he stood up from the table and complimented me for not drinking wine. He pointed to the bottle and told me he had the bad habit of always drinking half a bottle of Chambertin. Then, as he strolled around the room, he spoke again about the Prussian army, which he already knew very well, and asked me about the military academies. How far did they go in the study of mathematics? He was surprised at the elementary level at which they stopped. Didn't they teach applied geometry? I myself had not learned this, but only later studied it in Paris.

That same evening, in the room next door, there gathered a number of ladies who had come from the surrounding country to pay their respects to the Emperor. At times his questions seemed strange to them and his speech was disjointed, which meant that his thoughts at the moment were far away. To the gentlemen, who were gathered in a great crowd, dressed in stockings and shoes, he said they should wear boots and spurs.

A ball was held for him in the theater, and the hall was so packed with people that only a tiny dance floor remained. He walked about and talked to a great many of the guests, but I heard nothing of his conversation, as I did not join the throng around him but spent most of my time in the street, ensuring that the guard did not all go into the ball at the same time, or leave their horses with the servants. They had to be ready to escort the Emperor as soon as he left the ball, but he spent a good few hours there, at least until midnight.

A few days later an a.d.c. from Prince Murat arrived with the news that Warsaw had been taken. The Emperor set off the following day; the guard of honor escorted him for three miles. Then he bad us farewell, and ordered General Dabrowski to give all the troopers a subaltern's commission. He made Uminski a lieutenant colonel, Suchorzewski a major, and Gorzewski, a former Prussian cuirassier, and me, he made first lieutenants.

General Dabrowski had already begun to form four regiments of line infantry and two of regular cavalry, in addition to a local militia. The Emperor himself made Sulkowski a colonel, for a namesake had been his aide in Egypt and had died at the Battle of the Pyramids. Then the following wealthy citizens, who had provided funds for clothing the regiments, were appointed colonels: Mielzynski, Lacki, Poninski and Garczynski. But to each regiment General Dabrowski appointed a lieutenant colonel (or grosmajor as the Prussians would say) from among his old legionaries and former staff officers, who were to organize and command the regiments in reality.

At the wish of my father I became a lieutenant in Prince Sulkowski's regiment[7] and was assigned to a voltigeur company, whose commander was Captain Puchalski, a veteran of the Kosciuszko rebellion. The subaltern in this company was Gorzewski, a very dedicated and good officer, with a soldier's heart; he had studied the military sciences well.

Our garrison was established at Gniezno, where we already had 2,000 recruits, for the most part volunteers, and all the officers we needed. I joined my company right away and took up my duties. The troops were organized, uniformed and taught basic drill in a very short time.

Our drill regulations were provided by General Dabrowski, translated from the French. Knowing the Prussian system, it was easy for me to learn these new regulations, which were far simpler and much better suited to the conduct of war. We received our muskets very quickly. They were of recent manufacture, taken from the Berlin arsenal from which the

---

7 Prince Sulkowski was the son of Elzbieta Przebedowska, the wife of the voivod of Malborg and sister of Princess Moszczenska, who was Chlapowski's grandmother. He was therefore Chlapowski's second cousin.

Prussians had not managed to evacuate them. The bayonets were really much too long for them, so later we exchanged these for French ones. We had been drilling without weapons, but as soon as our muskets arrived, the recruits learned more easily how to march and trim their lines. I think it is pointless to tire out a recruit and waste time teaching him the so-called way of the soldier when he hasn't got a weapon; with a musket on his shoulder his bearing straight away improves, and it even becomes easier to keep regular formation.

We had a cheerful existence in Gniezno; drill all morning and French lessons after lunch. In the evening, after roll-call [apel], the officers were taught tactical theory by Lieutenant Colonel Majaczewski, and the n.c.o.s by Major Rogalinski.

French units marched through the town almost daily. Prince Sulkowski entertained their officers hospitably. There were also frequent parties in the barracks, or at the home of the Lieutenant Colonel whose wife and daughters were with him. The artillery also used to invite us to dinner and receptions.

Finally the order came to march out. The winter was mild but wet. We had copied the French infantry's custom of wearing light footwear, that is instead of boots, we wore shoes and low gaiters, which fit so tightly that the circulation is contained and the leg does not swell from fatigue. It is true that when marching in mud and snow they get wet easily, but at night in the barracks or by the fire in bivouac, they dry far quicker than boots, which also get wet through after a day's march through mud, and are far harder to dry out. While the gaiters, socks and shoes are drying by the fire, you can put on the set dried out the previous night, for it is far easier to have a spare pair of gaiters and shoes than to have spare boots, which stay damp for longer. It is sometimes said that shoes come off the foot more easily in deep mud, but this can only happen when the gaiters are badly fitted. When they do fit properly, shoes stay on even better than boots.

The top priority for infantry is to have healthy feet, and for this it is a great help to rub them with spirit [vodka] at night when you change footwear, for this not only guards against swelling, but also protects the foot against blisters. Our people like to smear tallow on their feet, especially when, instead of wearing socks, they bind them in canvas: you must not let the soldiers do this, as if the binding is not even, it will easily blister the foot. Soldiers should have three pairs of socks, which they should wash as often as possible. I am talking so much about infantrymen's feet because on these depend rapid marches, and it was a wise general who said, "Victory is in the legs."

On the march we collected regular rations of bread, meat, grits or pease pudding, and vodka. From Gniezno as far as Gniew we were billeted on the peasants. Our cook was a voltigeur who had been chef in some manor house. One day our captain fell ill. We left him behind, and never saw him again. He was, after all, already advancing in years. So from now on I commanded the company, and my subaltern was a very good second-in-command. When we were not camped too far apart, we normally ate together with the four non-commissioned officers and the duty orderlies. This was a habit we picked up from the French.

I had with me a servant, whom my father had sent with me, who rode my horse and looked after my portmanteau. I never rode on horseback, but always marched with the company, as did Second Lieutenant Gorzewski, who did not even want to have a horse. The marches were quite long, about four miles a day, through Gasawa, Bydgoszcz, Swiecie and Gniew. In Gniew, General Dabrowski caught up with us. He took some battalions out into the countryside and ordered them to perform certain manoeuvres. The movements in column went well, but battalions moving at the double in line with bayonets fixed were still very uneven and fell into bad disorder. The soldiers were not experienced enough yet to follow their marker with their eyes only, but instead turned their heads to the side as well. Once a few had turned their heads, their bodies could no longer walk in a straight line, steps became uneven and the whole line broke up as files either collided or diverged.

That same evening I was ordered to march without delay to Cieplo, where our advance guard stood, half a mile from Gniew in the direction of the Vistula. Snow was falling thickly, the roads and paths were already covered and the march was dreadful. When we reached Cieplo I reported to Major Suchorzewski, whose command of 150 horsemen manned the outposts. He allocated one of the three buildings to my company. The other two, a barn and a stable, were occupied by the lancers and their horses. The inhabitants were all Poles, who were very hospitable, but we were too crowded to be comfortable. Those soldiers who were not on guard occupied the main room, while I took over the bed chamber for we two officers and the three sergeants. I went straight out to place my detachments and pickets, with the help of the Major who had reconnoitered the area during the day. This was our first time so close to the enemy.

The Major told me that there were enemy hussars and jagers circling on the far bank of the Vistula, but I could not see them as the night was dark and the snow kept falling. We spent a whole day there, and in the evening I received orders to march to Mlynow, two and one half miles to the left. We only arrived at dawn, because we could only march very slowly, trudging in the dark behind our guide, through deep snow. On the high ground to the left of the village, I could see the fires of our whole division. Soon an officer came to meet me, with orders to report to General Dabrowski. I found him lying fully clothed on some straw in a hovel. He sent me off with Lieutenant Colonel Hurtig, who, instead of taking us towards the camp, led me and my company off to the right of the village into the undergrowth, and ordered me to camp and place my sentries there. We were to light fires for the soldiers to cook at.

I had read various manuals on the art of skirmishing, and was of the opinion then, as I am still today, that the Austrian light horse is the best trained in this kind of warfare. The Austrians are always the most skilled at placing outposts to guard their army.

And so I placed my sentries as I thought best on the high ground and returned to the company which, meanwhile, had been building fires and starting to cook in the low ground. The locals must have grown potatoes there once, but these had long since been dug up.

I settled down into a hollow to protect me from the wind, and covered my head with my greatcoat collar, or rather it was a fur-lined surtout, as it would be difficult to march in a greatcoat. I slept peacefully for a few hours, and the subaltern, on whom I could rely and who had taken the first rest, changed the guard.

The next day an officer from the Staff brought orders to join my regiment. I learned from him that our whole division had marched to the left towards Mlynow, because a Prussian corps had left Gdansk [Danzig] in order to cut off Prince Michal Radziwill's Northern Legion, and prevent it from joining us, but the Legion had defeated this attempt without our help and had entered Starogrod.

The Legion numbered 3,000 soldiers, all of them Prussian soldiers captured at Jena. All their officers were veterans who had come up with Dabrowski from Italy.

We returned once more to the Gdansk road, not to Gniew, but to a village outside the town, the name of which I forget, because my company was sent straight away to the advance guard.

This was commanded by Jan Dabrowski, the son of the General, and stood at Sulkowa, one and a half miles from Tczew. I was ordered to halt just behind the village. The peasants, who were all Poles, brought us more than enough to eat. The next day, it was still dark when General Dabrowski arrived, and an officer on his staff ordered me to march my company through the village and form up before it.

There I found the General surrounded by his senior officers, the old codgers as our wits would call them, to whom he was issuing orders for the attack on Tczew. As commander of the voltigeur company, I was ordered to join the circle, to hear the dispositions. The General ordered me to march close behind the leading cavalry squadron, which was to move to the side just as it reached the gardens of the town's suburbs, while I, having despatched half my company under my second lieutenant into the gardens in skirmish order, was to lead the other half past the houses on the edge of town and make for the so-called Vistula Gate, which our battalion with the grenadiers at its head was to take by storm. Our second battalion was detailed to take the so-called Mill Gate. Meanwhile, the cavalry was to circle round the town to the left and cover the Gdansk Gate, to attack the enemy as he made his escape.

General Dabrowski issued these orders very clearly, so all of us could understand. The advance began at once and lasted two hours. When the town came into view, and we caught sight of Prussian Hussars on the heights around it, we quickened our pace. Mounted skirmishers of both sides exchanged a few carbine and pistol shots, which, as usual with cavalry fire, wounded no one. When we reached the outskirts and the squadron to my front moved off at a trot to the left, I sent my second platoon into the gardens, and led the first platoon at the double up the street towards the town. The second platoon kept abreast of us on both sides, picking their way through the gardens.

The Prussians allowed us to get close to the first houses, and then, from windows, doors and loopholes in the walls, fired a single volley into my half-company. My sergeant, who was on my left, was mortally wounded, a few soldiers fell behind me and a good many more were wounded. The first volley had a dreadful effect on us, and we fled in disorder, leaving the dead and severely wounded where they lay. I confess that at that moment I lost my head. My sergeant, whose name was Moroh, had fallen so suddenly that I was quite sickened.

Seeing him laying there with his white face and lifeless body, I lost control. In short, we ran perhaps 150 paces to the rear, until we came upon our grenadier company at the head of the battalion. I then rallied my men and set off again in front of the battalion towards the houses. But the Prussians had not waited for the whole battalion to attack. As we ran through the streets in the outskirts, we could see them retreating before us. Covering their retreat were a few cavalrymen, whom we tried to catch, but they made it into the town and shut the gate. We were then about a hundred paces from the gate when a hail of bullets fell among us from the loopholes in the gate and from the houses lining the wall to its right.

A number of our men were hit, and then our lieutenant colonel, Sierawski, rode up and ordered us to shelter behind the nearest houses, saying, "Wait here, a cannon is on the way to batter open the gate." He, meanwhile, stayed in the street, and laughed when the bullets tore holes in the broad skirt of his dark blue greatcoat. Watching from my hiding place behind a house, I was very impressed by this display of nerve. After a few minutes, as slowly as you please, he turned and rode back to the battalion, which had also taken shelter by companies in the houses behind us. And so the street was left empty, but the initial firing had hit several soldiers as well as Lieutenant Colonel Muchowski, and the aide, Major Jozef Bojanowski, who was badly wounded. The wounded, including eleven men of my company, were evacuated under fire.

A good half hour passed before a cannon, with French crew, arrived and unlimbered. In front of it came some old French officer, riding beside Dabrowski's aide, Bergenzoni, who was hit immediately by an enemy bullet and fell off his horse just level with the house behind which we were huddled. The Frenchman did not even stir, as if he had not noticed his companion fall beside him. He stood so close to the cannon that the blast of its first round knocked his fine hat over his eyes.

"COME ON, YOUNG MAN, EARN YOURSELF A CROSS. INTO TOWN WITH YOU!"
THE GUN BLOWING DOWN THE GATE AT TCZEW

At the third shot the gate gave way and this officer said to me in French "Come on, young man, earn yourself a cross.[8] Into town with you!" We rushed forward and burst into the town, right in amongst the Prussians, who were no longer defending themselves, and we chased them as far as the main square, with the rest of the battalion right behind. I was thereupon

8   The French Cross of the Legion of Honor, for which Napoleon had decreed Polish troops were also eligible.

ordered to make for the other side of town, and a company was sent after the Prussians down a street to the right. I later learnt that they had taken shelter with their commander in the church, where they surrendered except for a few who had escaped across the thin ice of the Vistula, but many of these probably drowned. In the church they captured General Roth and about 800 men, mainly from a regiment of volunteer jagers; that explained why they had fired so effectively from the windows and gate and killed over 150 men from our battalion.

As soon as I found myself on the far side of the town, I was ordered to advance another half mile up the road to Stamberg, a small village of six small shacks, and to place a line of outposts and sentries between there and the Vistula.

That first engagement at Tczew made me realize that young soldiers who have not yet seen fire should not be broken up into skirmish order. It is safer to hold them in ranks in small detachments, with an officer commanding each. With such detachments placed wide apart, one can cover as much frontage as one would with skirmishers working in pairs.

General Dabrowski had been with our 2nd battalion during that engagement, and was wounded. General Kosinski took acting command, and a few days later General Geilgud, the hunchback, who was his senior, came to take over.

The 2nd battalion had broken into the town with Prince Sulkowski almost at the same time as ours, so as we had reached the main square we had seen it coming down one of the streets.

During the march to Stamberg we heard strong artillery and small arms fire about a mile off, ahead and to the right of the Gdansk road. We discovered some hours later that a Prussian column had marched from Gdansk to help Tczew, but General Menard and his Northern Legion had intercepted it from Starogrod, and forced it to retire. The firing did not last longer than an hour.[9]

When we reached Stamberg I scouted the area, and placed two outposts because there were two causeways. One of them carried the road to the next village, which we could see a mile away over the Zulawy water meadows, and the second went straight to the Vistula. They left Stamberg at sharply diverging angles, and then ran more or less parallel. At that time of year you can only cross the Zulawy along the causeways, as the meadows between them are covered with water. When I left Tczew, I had been given command of the 2nd battalion's voltigeur company, whose captain had been wounded, so I had a total of 200 men from both companies plus 50 sharpshooters whose captain, Golaszewski, had been killed. So I had 254 men under my command. On each causeway I placed 40 men, to defend the two approaches to the village. These outposts placed two sentries each, 200 paces in front of their positions by day, and 100 paces by night.

The next day, as it became clear that we would stay there for a few days, we brought up some wagons and old planks of wood that we had found in the village, and built barricades across the causeway in front of each outpost, with shelters behind, to protect the soldiers from bad weather and from sudden attack. And so, although the village was only a few hundred paces behind the outposts, we could rest peacefully in its houses.

I changed the outposts every twelve hours, at midnight and midday, so that everybody might have time to cook their meals in the buildings. Each day, before dawn, we would always stand to arms, until daybreak.[10] That was my absolute order. We did not need to stand to during the day, as in the completely flat region of the Zulawy you can see for miles around.

---

9 The Poznan Gazette reported on 21 March that General Dabrowski had awarded 14 crosses of the Legion of Honor for the attack on Tczew, including Chlapowski and one Charlet, officer of the French artillery.
10 To guard against a surprise attack at this, the most common time for nighttime assaults.

General Kosinski would visit our position several times during the day and night and always complimented me on the good order. We stayed there for four days and got a good rest. The enemy did not show himself; only on the fifth day did the outposts see some horsemen in the next village. This village, Zblewo, was nearly a mile from Stamberg. The cavalry could only travel along the causeways because the countryside was flooded. I took six soldiers from the outpost and advanced about 1,000 paces beyond our sentries. From there I could make out that there was infantry in Zblewo. As soon as we got back to Stamberg I sent a sergeant on a peasant's horse with a report back to Tczew.

Early the next morning, I was sent 30 French sappers, commanded by a sergeant, and ordered to take these men and my two companies and eject the enemy from Zblewo. I did not want to divide my forces, as whether in a major operation or a minor skirmish you should keep your force united as far as possible. I left a detachment of 30 men under Second Lieutenant Gorzewski to man the barricade on the left hand causeway. I knew I could rely on him as he proved himself under fire at Tczew. I was also confident, because I knew that only cavalry could be sent along this left hand causeway to outflank us, as infantry would be too slow. So I marched off with the rest of my force, and selected an advance guard from my Polish troops. But the French straight away requested permission to lead off, very politely explaining that older soldiers should set an example. I had wanted to keep them in reserve, which would have been the text book thing to do, but, as they insisted, I attached 30 men from my company to them, joined them myself, and ordered the main body to advance 200 paces behind us. I sent the French sergeant with five sappers and five of our men 100 paces out in front. These Frenchmen moved so fast that my men had difficulty keeping up.

We reached the edge of the village in under an hour and a few volleys were fired at the five sappers and five voltigeurs. At the same time I saw a few score hussars leave the village and set off along the left hand causeway. They were soon well behind our left rear, but as I was sure Gorzewski could hold these horsemen from behind his barricades, I attacked briskly with my first detachment, charged right through the village and stopped at the far side. A few shots still fell around and about us, but soon the sapper sergeant and his advanced party of ten men disappeared from view, so fast did they pursue the enemy. I also saw the hussars retreating along the causeway to the left, and I later learned that a number of them had been wounded and carried off by their companions.

As the Frenchman and his men were still nowhere to be seen, I called for two peasant's horses, mounted one, and ordered a soldier to mount the other. We set off at as fast a trot as these fat old horses could manage, and caught up with the Frenchman almost as he reached the next village. I turned him around and we retraced our steps. Zblewo is a big village, with good houses in the peasant style, with second floors in the eaves. The farmers were German, but they spoke Polish as their servants and maids were all Poles. These latter were delighted to see us, but the farmers also, no doubt out of fear, brought the soldiers food and drink in plenty. So anyway, I returned to Zblewo with the sergeant. I did not leave him to come back on his own, as he was fired up with anger and wanted to kill or capture himself a Prussian, and was so disappointed that he was returning "empty-handed" as he called it, that I was half afraid he would not come back.

I halted in Zblewo. While my men ate, I began writing my report to General Kosinski, but was informed that a few hundred of our infantry were marching toward us from Stamberg. They were two companies of Poninski's 12th Regiment, who had orders to support me if I needed them. Their captain had orders instructing me, if I succeeded in ejecting the enemy from Zblewo, to march straight away for Skarszew [Schoeneck], where our regiment was now stationed, and to send the sappers back to Tczew.

Our regiment had already reached Skarszew that morning, but I only reached there with my two voltigeur companies during the night. We found our quarters already prepared for us; Prince Sulkowski had made Captain Stanislawski the billeting officer there. This officer had spent many years in France and although he spoke German, he did so with a strong French accent.

He was always very friendly toward me, and had chosen comfortable quarters for us. He told me that the German inhabitants were very afraid of him because they thought from his accent that he was a Frenchman.

As the reader will recall, this area had been in Prussian hands for a good few decades, that is, since the first Partition in 1772. There had been a considerable influx of Germans, but not as many as I had expected. You could tell everywhere that they did not feel altogether at home. That was strange, as usually Germans easily become attached to the land that feeds them. Every nation has its own habits in this regard. Some people, if forced by events to leave their home country, always pine for it and do not settle happily elsewhere. But the German people always uproot without regret, and on the contrary will settle wherever they see a chance to improve their lot, without a backward glance. Moreover, without losing their racial identity, they are happy to respect the local laws of their new homeland, as long as this maintains order. I had several Germans from Leszno in my company. I even made one of them a non-commissioned officer and was very content with him. These men were less able to endure hardships than our Polish men, and so took greater care of themselves in everything which could preserve their health. In Gniezno, when they first joined us, they did not speak Polish, but soon learnt it well and were always our equals in the thick of battle. I made sure my Poles did not make fun of them and always treated them as comrades. I noticed more than once that they would carry muskets for the Germans when they were tired, to ease their load.

In the villages of this region the inhabitants are Poles, while there are lots of Germans in the small towns. But these can speak Polish, and hire Poles as farmhands and maids because they are hardier than Germans and will turn their hand to any kind of work, without complaining that it is not what they were hired to do.

After two days we marched two miles closer to Gdansk [Danzig], to the village of Zulawek, where we found our advance guard. As we approached the village we could see our piquets on the surrounding hills. These were troopers from Dziewanowski's lancers. They were surveying the countryside all around, and had piquets to the rear of the position as well. Colonel Dziewanowski had formed this regiment in Bydgoszcz from the so-called Prussian Companion Regiment,[11] which had come over to us almost in its entirety at Fordon, as soon as it had seem our army from the far bank of the Vistula. It was a well drilled unit as well. This regiment had contained a few officers and non-commissioned officers from Kosciuszko's old Polish army, who straight after the Partition of the country had passed with the entire regiment of "Golden Freedom" into Prussian service, finding themselves in Augustow, which Prussia had seized. To these 600, Dziewanowski added 300 recruits from Bydzgoscz, and thus a beautiful new regiment was created in its entirety. The uniforms of this, the only lancer regiment in the Prussian Army, had been of Polish cut, with dark blue kurtka, crimson facings and, so I was told, even red and white lance pennants.

11 The Towarczy (Polish for Companion) ulan regiment in Prussian service.

20

The village of Zulawek is tidily and prettily laid out. It belongs to some gentleman whose name I should not have forgotten, as he received us very hospitably. He was an old man who had been appointed chamberlain to Frederick II, but he never went to Berlin. Straight after the first Partition of our country, most of the Polish citizens had abandoned their possessions as worthless. Some had even given them to their servants, and themselves moved to parts of Poland which were still independent. Frederick II used various means to force the gentry to leave, and repopulated the villages with his Brandenburgers.

From Zulawek we marched another three miles to the outskirts of Gdansk. After marching for two of these we could see every road to the right and left, crowded with regiments marching on the city. We were virtually in the centre with Dziewanowski's lancers in front and a French battery behind us. To our right the advance was led by the 2nd French Light Infantry Regiment, and behind this, a Saxon division. To our left marched the 10th French Chasseurs à Cheval, followed by a battery and infantry brigade from Baden. Further to the left again was Radziwill's Northern Legion, and in front of it General Sokolnicki's cavalry, which had been recruited from the levies of Poznan and Kalisz. This great formation was a lovely sight. From time to time our cavalry scouts fired pistol shots. Only a few enemy cannon fired on us. I did not see any battery from our side leave the column of march, let alone unlimber.

Our division halted near Bomfield, but shortly after our regiment marched off to the left to the village of Schoenfeld, and there we made camp for the night. As soon as it grew dark, a massive fire broke out. The enemy had set light to the buildings outside the city walls. They burned all night, and it was so bright in our camp that we could read by their light.

We spent two days at Schoenfeld, and on the third we swapped positions with the 12th Regiment and moved to the village of Kowal. Every two days we swapped around, I know not for what reason, as in both places we camped in the open, and only the headquarters were in shelter. The air was mild, but the ground was covered with snow. We had enough straw for shelter and to lie on, and received regular rations. Not one of us fell sick. A man adapts easily to life beneath the stars, and need suffer no hardships from it, and time passes cheerfully in the company of good comrades. We placed sentries in front of our camps, and my turn to do duty came round from time to time. I especially recall the 12th of March, a rotten night to be on sentry duty, as we had sorted out our roster and lit our fires, when Lieutenant Colonel Cedrowski arrived, bringing me an order to occupy the burned suburb of Schotland, where I was forbidden to light fires so as not to alert the enemy. There, with neither straw nor fire, we spent a whole soggy night, jumping up and down in the mud and snow to keep warm. I posted piquets very close to our position, as the night was dark. In fact the whole company stood to arms, as none of us dared lie down. I cannot remember a worse night in this whole war. Only around dawn some soldiers brought us some planks from the burned buildings, on which Gorzewski and I took turns to rest, for we could not lie on the ground as it was knee-deep in mud and slush. I shall never forget that night, which seemed interminable to me, and I describe it in detail so that young soldiers know what to expect of war: not just bullets, but discomfort, for which they must be prepared. Actually good company reduces the suffering, and our soldiers did not complain. I even heard some singing an old military song of ours from the days of Kosciuszko, which begins:

"Be he in battle or be he in camp,
A soldier is happy as if at a dance."
Yet I heard others say: "Cold, hungry, and a long way from home."

At about 9 A.M., as we were expressing surprise that we had not been relieved, our whole regiment marched up to join us, and together we advanced right up to the outskirts of the city. We halted in a fold in the ground. The 12th Regiment passed by and advanced further. We were ordered to rest arms and await orders.

Soon a lively exchange of small arms fire broke out to our front. Within an hour, the 12th Regiment was master of the district of Stolzenberg.

The enemy retired to the Biskupia Gora [Bishop's Hill], and from that fortification opened fire with their artillery. The 12th Regiment lost many men that day, as the enemy hidden behind the fortified buildings could fire from safety. The wounded were brought back near us, and cannon balls flew past but over our heads. This was a useful experience for us: all our soldiers could see that the balls flying overhead were not hitting us, for although we were close, we were on much lower ground. We were reassured by this, and able to confirm the saying that you can only hear the roar or whistle of a cannon ball if it is missing you. On the other hand, you cannot hear the shot which hits you at all.

Four companies of the 12th Regiment remained in Stolzenberg, which had also been nearly burned to the ground, and the rest withdrew to Kowal. Our regiment retired to Wonnenberg, where we made camp, and were able to make cooking fires for the first time in twenty-four hours.

I think few of my company had so much as eaten a chunk of bread in that twenty-four hours. We were inexperienced soldiers and had kept no rations with us. I mention this to teach those who are starting out on military service, that they should always have a bit of bread with them for emergencies. Everyone should remember this lesson.

On 17th March we began digging trenches for the siegeworks. In the evening I was sent with my company to protect a French engineer officer and 40 sappers. As soon as it got dark, the sappers started work.

FRENCH SAPPERS AT WORK

FRENCH INFANTRY CARRYING GABIONS

In the night the enemy sent out patrols towards our front line from the forts of Biskupia Gora and Gradowa Gora. When they heard the sound of digging they opened up with small arms fire. Soon they fired two flares to light up the place where they had heard the digging and directed their artillery fire at this point. The trench had been started between the foundations of some houses at the foot of the escarpment; before it became deep enough to shelter in, one of my soldiers was wounded and one sapper killed. But by dawn the work was so far advanced that when daylight arrived and the enemy increased his fire, we could already lie concealed at the bottom of the trench. The shot so peppered the front lip of the trench that we had to keep piling it up again. During the day we positioned gabions, filled them with earth and in this way strengthened the position. The sappers should have placed the gabions right at the start, but these had only arrived during the day with a second unit of sappers.

About a thousand paces beyond the range of the forts' cannon, the rest of our division stood to arms behind us to dissuade the enemy from attempting a sortie to disrupt the building of the siege works. I later learned that digging had also begun at two other points in the line.

The following day another company came to relieve mine, but as it was already daylight when they approached, they were greeted on the road with enemy shells, as were we when we marched away to our camp by Wonneberg. However, nobody was hurt.

Thereafter, movements to and from the siegeworks took place after dusk and before dawn, so that the fortress would have more difficult targets to hit.

When we were in camp at Wonneberg we heard firing night and day, if not to our front, then to our right where the Saxons were, or to the left among the Badeners. They too were building siegeworks, but we could not see these from the Wonneberg. Neither could we see our company working with the sappers. Half way between our camp and the siege lines four companies stood under arms around the clock. They changed every twenty-four hours. The company in the trenches changed every twelve hours as they were helping the sappers in their work and moreover could not sleep there. In addition, every day the whole regiment stood to arms before dawn and remained so for an hour or so, until day had finally broken. Despite the precautions, the enemy made a sortie from the Gradowa Gora against the Badeners, ejected them from their trenches, and seized the heights of the Cyganska Gora, opposite the Gradowa fort. A few hundred cossacks fell upon the Badeners as they ran away from the trenches, and captured I do not know how many. Some French Chasseurs a Cheval appeared but retired in confusion, no doubt because this was their first sight of cossacks. Also perhaps because they were only a small unit. From the Wonneberg, where we were standing under arms, we could only see one face of the Cyganska heights, but we had a good view of it and watched as two squadrons of Saxon dragoons then advanced resolutely on the Cossacks, who retreated into the fortress. The Chasseurs had been deployed in skirmish order and so the Cossacks had not retired before them, but they immediately ran from the Dragoons in line formation.

On the 22nd Marshal Lefebvre came to inspect us, made a speech, and ordered us to perform some drill. When we stood in line, he rode with his staff up and down between the ranks. Then he ordered the center companies of each battalion[12] to form column. The four companies to our front were then ordered back to the battalion, reformed back into line and we were then instructed to advance at the double with bayonets fixed. Then we formed squares in normal three-deep formation, and finally "full" squares, which left three "roty"[13] per company to the rear, to fill any gaps between the companies. We thus carried out all the manoeuvres which are really vital for use in battle. They were performed quite well, despite the mud and snow.

That day the Marshal brought his headquarters from Pruszcz to Pickendorf, to a more central position in the siegeworks. The fortifications of Gdansk, which are made of several smaller strongpoints, are easier to besiege than first appears, for although the perimeter is very great, most of it is bounded by the Vistula and the flood plains of the Zulawy, which at this time of year are impassable. Besides this, you only need to assault the city from the south, because on this side stand both of the city's major forts, the Gora Biskupia and Gora Gradowa. Even if the city was occupied from the other side, these forts could survive and fight independently, and the attackers could not remain in the city, as from these heights the enemy could turn it into a hell. So there is no need to occupy the whole perimeter, only half of it, and the parallels need only be dug from the south. Once the Biskupia and Gradowa Goras are taken, the city can no longer defend itself. On the other side of the Vistula to the east, where a communication bridge is always needed to link Pruszcz and the spit of sand that stretches along the sea to Pitawa, it is wise to place a corps of observation. If this corps is strong enough, it should size the island of Holm, standing between the Vistula and the canal, and in this way cut Gdansk's communications with the forts of Weichselmunde and Fahwasser at the mouth of the Vistula, and hence with the sea.

So our division was right in the center of the siege lines. To our right the Saxon division, to our left the Baden brigade, and the Northern Legion on the extreme left flank. In Langfur,

12 The Polish battalion organization was 4 center companies, one grenadier and one light company.
13 A "rota" was a file of three soldiers. The three roty behind each company was to plug gaps caused by casualties.

General Sokolnicki's cavalry brigade occupied an arc facing west with its left flank on the sea. In the early days, when the city was not yet hard-pressed by us, this brigade had frequent tussles with the enemy which made sorties from the western side of the city.

The first and second parallels in front of the Biskupia and Gradowa Goras progressed so quickly that work soon began to install the battery of heavy cannon. The sappers did most of their work at night, but even then the enemy cannon fired with good effect, always lighting up the area with illuminating flares. Their marksmen would also advance right up to our pickets, which were of course close to our main body at night time; and as soon as a flare revealed the sappers placing gabions and filling them with earth they would open fire, but with little result.

On 26 March it was again the turn of my company to guard the trenches. At 4 A.M. I had relieved a company of the 12th Regiment, and we had hardly had time to deploy in the trench and allocate sentry duties when a hail of musket fire

MARSHAL LEFEBVRE

opened upon us from our left. Although it was still dark, the snow made visibility easier, and I caught sight of enemy skirmishers skirting round our left flank to take us from the rear. The Badeners must have either surrendered without a fight or run away, I do not know which, for the enemy was already several hundred paces beyond the Badeners' trenches and almost behind us. We moved fast; beyond the skirmishers a column of enemy infantry was marching around our left flank, and more skirmishers were now attacking us from the front. It was too late to retreat directly on our supporting companies as we had been ordered to do in case of a surprise attack, so we retreated to our right, toward Stolzenberg. The devastated quarter of Stolzenberg was on higher ground to our right, and the trenches there were manned by companies of the 10th and 11th Regiments. We picked our way through gardens and over walls toward them, with bullets flying around us from the pursuing skirmishers. But we had not gone half way when we saw that Stolzenberg was already held by enemy infantry, which greeted us with a brisk volley. Luckily because of the darkness, only a few of us were hit. We had no choice but to run back through the gardens, under fire now from both directions. Leaving the gardens, we again turned to the right, and dragging and supporting our wounded, we made our way toward our four supporting companies, who were advancing to our assistance. Major Malczewski, who was in command, rode up to us on horseback followed

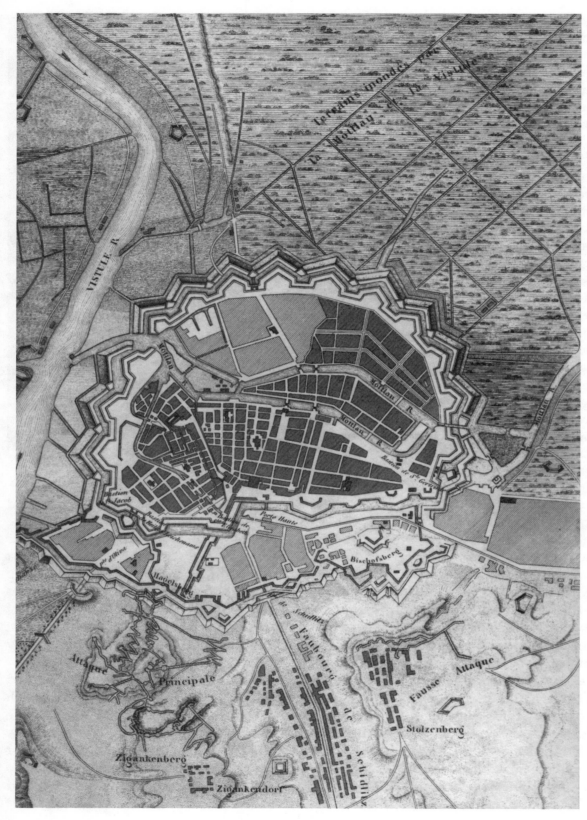

MAP OF THE SIEGE OF GDANSK

by several skirmishers. They turned back the enemy who had attacked us from behind. The major began leading us back to his four companies, but from his horse he could see whole columns of enemy marching out from the city (it was getting lighter by then), and so ordered his command to turn about and retire to Wonneberg. As I and my men were still 100 or 150 paces behind, he ordered us to stay in skirmish order and cover their retreat.

We retreated a few hundred paces towards Wonneberg, with the four companies in column and mine skirmishing 150 paces behind them, firing back at the cloud of cossacks which had swarmed out ahead of their infantry. Behind the cossacks, I soon caught sight of regular cavalry deploying for action. At that, I summoned my company to form up, and keeping a dozen men with me, I ordered the sub-lieutenant to retreat with the main body in formation, while I and my little band followed about 50 paces behind. But it was already too late. Two squadrons of enemy dragoons formed line. One charged right into and through us. I fell between two horses, struck in the throat.

I lost consciousness, and do not know how long I lay there, nor did I know who stripped my uniform off me. When I came to, I was lying on the ground surrounded by a group of cossacks. Only one of my voltigeurs was nearby; he had lost his overcoat, but not his uniform. A cossack officer ordered me to stand, but I could not raise myself as my neck and shoulder were stiff. He gave me his hand and helped me up, ordered one of his cossacks to dismount and put me on his horse. He led it, without giving me the reins, through the destroyed outskirts, between the Biskupia and Gradow Goras, through Stiglitz and into the city. Once through the gate the Cossack helped me dismount and onto a bench, where I sat with my teeth rattling from the cold, as I was undressed. A cossack colonel rode up, dismounted and gave me a nip of vodka. He asked four of the cossacks present what uniform I had been wearing, and within a quarter of an hour he returned it to me, still with the ribbon of the Legion of Honor, but without the cross. I had been awarded the cross for the assault on Tczew; Marshal Lefebvre's chief of staff, who had been by the gates of Tczew when we stormed it, had pinned it on me a few days after. My czapka had gone missing, but the colonel gave me a cossack's cap. It was better than nothing. We joined some other prisoners who had already been brought in: Lieutenant Sokolowski from one of the four supporting companies, which I learned had been broken; one French soldier; four men from my company; one officer of engineers and one of artillery, both French; and finally a Baden officer and a dozen or so of his men. The French soldier, who was from the 2nd Light Infantry Regiment, was surrounded by Prussian officers. As they could speak French they were talking with him; he was very talkative, unlike the two French officers who refused to answer any questions. This soldier of the 2nd Light gave one answer which later became widely known. One of the Prussian officers said that Frenchmen only fight for money. The Frenchmen boldly replied: "And what do you fight for?"

"We fight for honor."

"Quite right too," he retorted, "every man fights to get what he lacks."

We were led to some kind of a stone building in the city, and after two days to Farwasser, where we were put on a Swedish ship[14] and taken to Pilawa, then to Klajpeda, and finally to Riga.

We spent six weeks at sea, very poorly nourished. Nearly all of us came down with scurvy. Uminski and Malet were also there with 200 soldiers.

---

14 Sweden was allied with Prussia and Russia at this point, and its forces took part in the defence of Danzig.

We made plans to take over the ship as the crew was weak, but we decided not to try anything as we were told that the war was nearly over.

In Riga we were quartered in the outskirts and given a half-pension. All the officers and men fell sick one after another with nervous fever because of the bad food on the ship. I was one of the last to fall ill. I lay unconscious for several days; I was saved by bleeding heavily from my nose and mouth.

Peace was made at Tilsit and we were freed. I took myself straight to Vilnius, where I knew I would find Mr. Michal Oginski, who I had known in Berlin. He welcomed me most graciously and lent me the money I needed to get back to Warsaw. I stayed with him for a few days and got to know the city. On my arrival I reported to the governor, General Korsakow, the same who had been beaten by Massena at Zurich. Korsakow was a friendly old man and invited me to dinner, at which he started talking about his campaign in Switzerland. When he saw that I knew all about that war, he spoke more openly about it. I gathered that the Lithuanians were content with him. I met a few Lithuanian gentlemen, and got to know Mr. and Mrs. Tyzenhauz particularly well. At last I left by post-chaise, as I could afford this luxury, and did not stop except for one day at Grodno to visit the area and the buildings there which have such dreadful memories for us.

I stayed a week in Warsaw in order to see everything and put my affairs in order. After reporting to Prince Jozef [Poniatowski) and our general staff I went home [to Poznan); I found my father in good health. There I received my appointment to become an orderly officer (officier d'ordonnance to the Emperor, and soon set off for Paris.

Although called orderly officers we were in fact the Emperor's aides de camp, as the generals who bore this title never carried out the duties of an a.d.c. Most often these were corps commanders, such as Junot, Marmont, Rapp, Savary, Bertrand, Mouton, Lauriston, Drouot,

THE SIEGE OF GDANSK AT NIGHT

28

PRISONER OF THE COSSAKS

Lebrun, Lemarais, Durosnel, and Caffarelli. When Marmont became a marshal, he was replaced by Narbonne, who was replaced in 1813 by Flahaut. Most often only two of these a.d.c.s would be with the Emperor, sometimes only one and occasionally none.

Because we were then at peace, I received permission from the Emperor to follow courses at the Ecole Polytechnique. So I rented rooms nearby and attended the courses, and between these and the course in advanced mathematics, about which the emperor had asked me in Poznan and I had been unable to reply, my time was fully taken up. In addition to mathematics, I attended courses at the Polytechnic on geology, chemistry, botany, engineering, and so on.

The Ecole Polytechnique at that time was without doubt the best military academy in Europe. It took the science of military theory to the greatest possible extent. The spirit of the students, young and old, was so good that they never talked of anything but their studies, even among themselves. But there was anyway very little time for such talk, because our co-repetitors would arrive at 6 A.M. to spend two hours going over what we had learnt before we went to the first lecture. So everyone had to be up and dressed before 6 A.M. Lessons went from 8 to 11 A.M., then a short meal, then lessons again from 12 to 5 P.M., dinner at 5, then from 7 to 10 the co-repetitors went over with the students what had been taught in the day. Sometimes they would sit until 11 or 12 P.M. with the less gifted pupils. They took their duties very seriously. During lunch and dinner war was the main topic of conversation, in which we would apply the theories we were learning to campaigns gone by. Everybody was convinced that experience was vital, but that experience without a military education was not enough to make general officers.

I would return every evening to my digs at the house of Doctor Markowski, who in the closing years of the free Polish state had been sent as one of the best minds at Krakow University to Paris to perfect his medical education. Our country was dismembered, the French Revolution erupted, and Markowski spent 26 years in Paris continually learning, and becoming the best of teachers. I urged him to go back to his homeland, for it was the duty of everyone to be of service to his country. But he only made up his mind in 1809. Another of our co-repetitors, Livet, also decided at my urging to go home, and later became professor of the school of applied sciences in Warsaw. Many of our engineer and artillery

GENERAL KOSCIUSZKO IN OLD AGE

officers owed a great deal to his lessons in applied mathematics, and I am sure several of them will remember him with gratitude.

I should add here that lessons at the Ecole Polytechnique were given by gentleman whose names are of worldwide renown: Monge, Foureroi, Faugeas de St. Fond Thenard, Tussieu, and others.

As you can imagine, we young men so encumbered with work, denied any light hearted pursuits, even in our free time talking of nothing else except the military sciences, made great progress in out studies. Only on Sundays, and not every week, a few of us would go to the theater, but always to tragedies as we were of a serious frame of mind. It is no surprise that graduates of the Ecole Polytechnique tended to give excellent service in later life.

During a break of a few days I went to Berville, outside Fountainebleu, to see General Kosciuszko. He lived with a friend, a Swiss gentleman called Zetnur, who had a house in Berville and some land on which our famous Commander-in-Chief practised farming. I found him in French peasant's costume, with a straw hat, a grey smock, short breeches, and thick stockings. He had already lost his front teeth, which distorted his speech. He was very kind to me, and told me all about the war he had waged. I recall that when he described to me the attack on the Russian battery at Raclawice,[15] he threw himself forward as if pushed by an invisible hand, as he cried "Forward! By God!", and he clamped his straw hat so firmly on his head that he crushed it completely. Undoubtedly he remembered that day so vividly that he clutched his straw hat just as he had gripped his Krakowian cap on the day of battle.[16]

He also described for me the wild mare which he was riding when at the end of the battle of Maciejowice she sank into the mud; he was captured, wounded by cossacks. He then said the following words, which I recall very clearly, concerning my position with the Emperor: "It is good that you are studying and learning. Study carefully, and when war breaks out, keep your eyes peeled. Being at the Emperor's side, you can gain great experience and knowledge. Learn and remember all you can, so this might one day be of use to your country. You are at a good school, but don't think, don't ever tell yourself that he [the Emperor] will resurrect Poland. He only thinks of himself, not about nationalist ideals, and so he could not care less about any dreams of independence. He is a despot, whose sole ambition is to satisfy his personal ambition. He will create nothing of any permanence, of that I am sure. But don't let this prevent a young man like you from gaining experience from him and learning his strategy. He is a great captain, and although he will not rebuild our country, he can train many of our officers, and it would be good if we had such men when God sends us the opportunity in future. I repeat, study carefully, but he will do nothing for us."

In May 1808 I received an order to report to the Emperor in Bayonne. I had only just passed my exam from the Ecole Polytechnique. I took it with General Bertrand, who was at that time the inspector of the engineers. He was gentle in his choice of question, and did not examine me as strictly as he would the real students, who had followed the whole course from the start.

---

15 Kozciuszko's victory over the Russian forces during the 1794 Rebellion, which came to symbolize the spirit of Polish insurrection. This battle saw a charge by Polish militia, armed with scythes, which overturned the center of the Russian position.

16 This soft, peakless cap had the square crown which later so distinguished the Polish military headdress, or czapka.

THE SPANISH CAMPAIGN OF 1808

I spent three days in Bayonne, just at the time when the old Spanish king, Charles IV, his queen, and the Prince of Peace [Godoy] were leaving for Valencay, where the Emperor was to imprison them. King Charles had fled his country after the revolution in Aranjuez, which had deprived him of his throne and placed the crown on the head of his son Ferdinand. The Emperor also invited Ferdinand to Bayonne, but refused to recognize him as king and packed him off to Valencay as well. Later, King Charles, his queen and the Crown Princess of Etruria left to live in Italy and only Ferdinand stayed in Valencay.[1]

The Emperor and Empress lived in the palace of Marac a quarter of a mile from the city on the road to Pamplona. It was not a large house. There was a large hall at its center, which one walked straight into from outdoors without passing through an entrance hall. This served as a mess for the staff officers when we were on duty. Leading off this hall on one side were two rooms, one in which the Emperor slept, and the other in which he dined with the Empress. On the other side there were another two room, both occupied by the Empress. Upstairs lived the ladies in waiting: the Empress's tutors, an Italian and two Irish women, and opposite them the ladies of the wardrobe. Marshal Berthier, the army chief of staff; Marshal Duroc; Archbishop Mechlinski (the Imperial chaplain); Secretary of State Maret; the Foreign Minister Champagny; the a.d.c.s General Mouton and Durosnel, later joined by General Bertrand; and Mr. Senfft Pisach, the Saxon plenipotentiary of whom the Emperor was so fond (his wife was with him, a charming and wise lady, if a little deaf), all lived in houses nearby belonging to the merchants of Bayonne.[2]

A battalion of Old Guard Grenadiers were camped in tents right by the chateau, so close that only a carriage could pass between them and the wall. Right beside them were 200 Basques from the Pyrenees, who had formed a guard of honor for the Emperor. Their costume was a short blue jacket, short black breeches, white stockings and gaiters, and a small dark blue woollen cap. They were a fine looking, lively people, and reputedly very good shots. Five hundred paces further on along the Pamplona road was a squadron of our [Polish Guard] Chevauxleger under Captain Dziewanowski. Whenever the Emperor went out on horseback or by carriage, an escort of 25 of these men and an officer would go with him.

---

1   Chlapowski's footnote in the Polish edition:
     Valencay was the palace of prince Talleyrand. He complained to the Emperor that it cost him more to maintain the King than he was being paid for, as Ferdinand had a large court with him. When the Emperor paid little attention to this complaint, Talleyrand said to him: "But what should I say to him?" (Mais que dois je lui dire alors?)"
     "Say mass to him." ("Dites lui la messe"), replied the Emperor.
     Talleyrand had of course been a priest and bishop before the Revolution, but had found it expedient to desert the Church.
2   Extract from the Memoirs of Count de Sentff Pisach, former Minister of Saxony, (in French in the Polish edition):
     "The Emperor was staying at the chateau of Marac, a quarter of a league from the Porte d'Espagne and Mr. de Champigny lived in a neighboring house. Mr. de Senfft arranged to live nearby. A squadron of the Polish Guard camped in a nearby wood provided the palace guard. The Vistula Legion and that fine regiment of lancers commanded by Colonel Konopska (sic) were the first troops to march out of the city and the lancers performed several pretty maneuvers before the terrace of the chateau. On their arrival in Bayonne Mr. and Mrs. de Senfft had received a laisser-passer for the palace, which amounted to an invitation to spend evenings in the Empress's apartments, where the dignitaries of the court would gather from half past nine to midnight. These were Mme de Montmorency and Mme Maret, the pretty Mme Garana who was tutor to the Empress, the Grand Marshal of the Palace (Duroc), General Ordener, equerry to the Empress, Generals Bertrand and Lebrun, who was son of the Imperial Treasurer, and a young Polish officer d'ordonnance called Chlapowski, to whom the Emperor had taken a fancy, and who at that time enjoyed a charmed life at court. The Polish deputies (voivods Stanislaw, Bilinski and Dzialynski) enjoyed the same privileges during their stay."

The Palace quartermaster allocated me lodgings at the house of M. Taubin, an old naval captain, a very good man, whose house was right on the edge of town by the so-called Spanish Gate. As it was clear we would be dealing one way or another with the Spaniards, I took on a Spanish teacher, who would arrive daily at 6 A.M. At 8 A.M. I had to report for duty, when, together with all the other officers, we would go into the Emperor's first room to receive our orders for the day. This took five to ten minutes, then we would go and sit in our duty room and each busied himself as he wished until ordered to attend on the Emperor. Most of us would read or chat. I often played chess with the Chamberlain, Bondy. At 11 A.M. we would go to eat with

THE EMPRESS JOSEPHINE

Marshal Duroc, whose house was closest to the chateau, and we would return straight to our room. A great many people would pass through that room during the day. Ministers with immense ledgers would wait there until the Emperor received them one after another in his office. Archbishop Pradt spent a good part of each day in there, and always had a lot of interesting gossip to tell. Every day numerous officers and couriers arrived from all directions. These would be brought before the Emperor by an a.d.c., but if none was present in the room, one of us orderly officers took their place.

At 3 or 4 P.M., before dinner which was regularly at 6 P.M., the Emperor normally went out horse riding, or in the carriage with the Empress, most frequently to the coast at Biarritz, a very beautiful spot. They were accompanied only by a driver on the coach, and followed by the detachment of 25 Polish light horse and one officer.

At 6 P.M. we would dine. The Emperor ate alone with the Empress, and they were sometimes joined by the Prince of Neuchatel. In the evening everyone would gather in the Empress's drawing room. The Emperor would join us only rarely. Sometimes he would walk around the room talking, and only the ladies were permitted to remain seated. At other times he would sit and order us to do the same. One day he came into the room with a little book in his hand and said, "What a bore, they can't even write a good novel. I have nothing to read, " and chucked the book onto a chair. It may seem surprising that this man had the time to read novels. It is good proof that he had organized an excellent administrative machine.

Some evenings we played cards, a game called "Krebs." Normally nobody won or lost, although the stakes were always in gold coin. As you can imagine, nobody played for the money and we all played without really concentrating. Yet one evening I won a few score napoleons and felt almost ashamed of myself for doing so, although I never paid more attention to the game than the other players. Only the Empress won often. Many of us would lose out of politeness, knowing it amused her to win. But she never gathered up her winnings when she left the table, which was normally before midnight. I never knew what happened to them afterwards. As soon as the Emperor and Empress made a move, we would all go.

Soon the Emperor sent me with some despatches to Spain.[3] I set off by post horse, and by nightfall, had reached the little river Bidassoa. Here the whole countryside and people were different. There can be no frontier in Europe which so starkly divides two such markedly different countries. Elsewhere the change is gradual, but here it is sudden. On one side of the Bidassoa the people are short, cheerful and lively, and on the other [Spanish] side, tall, serious and dreary. On the French side, little houses with cheerful gardens are scattered here and there, over more or less flat countryside, while on the far side stands the town of Irun, hewn from the local stone, with high mountains behind it into which the road climbs immediately on leaving the town, twisting and turning upwards from peak to peak until it reaches Vittoria, 33 Spanish leagues, or 24 Polish miles away.

There was a post rider, a Spaniard in his great cape, galloping along in front of me. His horse's bridle was covered with bells, so at night, although I could not see him, I could always hear him. Spanish post horses are marvellous mounts, able to gallop both uphill and down, so they can maintain a speed of two and a half miles an hour. I reached Vittoria at dawn, Burgos by midday, and then Madrid on the second day. But by then I could no longer feel my limbs and had to be carried in to the Marshal, as I could not stand.

After I handed him his orders I was taken to a post house with a very good bed, and was given a servant. The Marshal's own aides helped me undress, but my feet were so swollen that nobody could pull off my boots. They had to be cut off me, even though in Bayonne I had chosen the broadest pair I could. I did not sleep at all the first night, as I had a temperature and still could not feel my limbs. But I was able to think clearly and was awake all night. I had the most dreadful headache. I had eaten nothing on the way, and had been thirsty only on the second day, when I had drunk sugared water at nearly every stop. On that second day, I had needed help mounting my horse, for I could no longer do this alone. Only after my second night in Madrid, which I slept right through, was I able to have a bath and eat an excellent breakfast. I was ready to return, but I was kept there for a few weeks.

I have described this journey for the benefit of young men who might find themselves having to ride non-stop for several days and nights. They will need very loose fitting boots, wooden bucket stirrups, and a long saddle with a notched leather surface. You shouldn't eat too much before setting off, and you won't want to eat while you are on the road. When riding by day in hot weather, your throat will feel dry, and you need a small flask of French cognac to sip, but not gulp. Every deep draught will magnify the fever which you will inevitably get after a 48 hour ride. In hot weather you should not drink water, in case you sweat and are weakened thereby. Just by wetting the throat with cognac, a man can refresh himself and gain new vigor.

On 2 May the Madrid uprising took place. It had been planned for 3 May to begin at that greatest of Spanish passions, a bullfight. All the French officers had been invited and were to be murdered there, to make it easier to finish off the soldiery later. There were no more than

---

3 The order read as follows (in French in the original)
"Orderly Officer Chlapowski will set off forthwith. He will arrange to arrive at Vittoria before 4 a.m. tomorrow. There, he will deliver the attached letter to General Verdier's staff. He will continue his journey to Burgos, without stopping, and will deliver the second letter to Marshal Bessieres. He will stay in Burgos until the Marshal releases him. Bayonne, 3 June 1808.

THE MADRID UPRISING

4,000 infantry in Madrid, the Fusiliers of the Guard, twelve artillery pieces and 200 Mamelukes at the royal palace. The cavalry of the Guard was stationed in villages 1 to 1z\x miles from the city, as there are no villages closer to Madrid. It is an empty country, which looks like a flat plain but is crisscrossed with ravines.

The conspiracy was quite well prepared. The ringleaders collected several thousand men from the two Kingdoms of Castile, who made their way by night along the ravines, avoiding the one road our army had constructed, until on the night of 2 May they were right outside the city. But on 1 May we got wind of the plot and the order went out that day that all French officers with quarters in the town should gather at the Buen Retiro hostel. The conspirators must have heard about this order and decided to start the rising up straight away. So that night they hastened the arrival of their countrymen, and at dawn on 2 May several thousand peasants burst into the town, surprised the guard by the gates, and made for the arsenal.

The inhabitants collected in the key areas around the city, armed with long swords and knives. Many had firearms. Most of them gathered in the city center at the square called the Puerto del Sol, but they were also milling around in the side streets. They shot at officers riding past with orders. Murat's a.d.c., Gobert, was stabbed several times in the legs as he fought his way through the Puerto del Sol (he was on a very tall horse), but despite this he made it right across town to the Fusiliers, who straight away marched to the arsenal. They took it without a shot and dispersed the crowd which had taken a few old artillery pieces, but did not know how to fire them. About 2,000 peasants and citizens were captured. There was an order to shoot any Spaniard caught with a weapon in his hand, and so after peace had been restored, that is, after no more than a couple of hours (even the cavalry only arrived as the uprising was petering out, so only the Mamelukes took part), these 2,000 prisoners were led out of the city, lined up beneath its wall, and the order given to a battalion of Fusiliers to shoot them. It fired on command and they all fell to the ground, but not one of them was even wounded. For the soldiers had fired into the air, either on orders, or because old soldiers don't like to fire on unarmed men, I don't know which. But the generals, knowing their soldiers' views on this, but not daring to disobey the Emperor's instructions, had simply given the order and left the officers and men to carry it out as they saw fit. The battalion marched away, and the Spaniards, realizing they were safe, scampered off to their homes.[4]

It is a strange thing that tens of thousands of people, nearly all of them armed, could not overwhelm a few thousand regular, experienced soldiers. Perhaps it's best explained by the fact that Spain had not been at war for many years, so lacked experienced officers to organize them.[5]

I came to know many Spanish gentlemen, and observed that for all that the populace was bold and ready to sacrifice itself, the grandees [the high nobility] were decadent. American gold and a long peace had spoiled them.

Among their officers there was one only, Palofax,[6] at that time a captain in the Regiment of the Calatrava horse guards, who seemed to be a man of energy, who was suffering deeply from the subjugation of his country to a foreign government.

Back in Bayonne I told the Emperor everything that I had seen in Spain. I did not hide from him my belief that once the whole population of Spain discovered what had happened to its royal family, and learned that instead of Ferdinand, the Emperor was sending his brother Joseph to be King, there would be a general uprising. The minor rebellion of 2 May in Madrid had been the work of only a few people, and the population had not known then that Ferdinand was already a prisoner in Valencay and would never return. Had they known this, the rebellion could not have been confined to the capital.

The Emperor had a clear and brisk way of asking questions, and my answers were equally frank. When I said I expected a general uprising, he questioned this assumption and asked me to explain my reasons. This I again did. During this interview the Empress had been sitting on a settee in the room. When I went to her salon that evening, she called me aside and advised me to be more careful in my comments to the Emperor, as he did not like it when his opinions were challenged. She added that I should have realized that the Emperor was not happy when I had spoken about an uprising. I thanked the Empress for her advice, but did not change my manner of reporting to the Emperor thereafter, and I never once felt I had displeased him. On the contrary, he was always kindly towards me right until the end of my service with him. This episode shows the Empress had a good heart, but was not, perhaps, very shrewd.

Soon after my return to Bayonne, nearly all the members of the Cortes came there from Spain. There were about a hundred of them. The President of the Cortes was Prince Infantado. Every day they were given banquets by M. Maret (Duc de Bassano), Champagny (Duc de Cadore), Duroc (Duc de Frioul) and the Saxon minister, M. Senfft Pisach, who with his slightly deaf but very witty wife kept a most pleasant salon, where we would often gather in the summer house of a Bayonne merchant. The Spaniards all stayed in the town.

4   A wishful account of an incident for which the French were vilified by the Spanish people. If a few were lucky enough to survive, the majority of the insurgents was gunned down by the firing squads.
5   Remember Chlapowski wrote from the standpoint of one who had participated in an initially successful insurrection against Russian occupation in 1830. Chlapowski must have felt some sympathy for the Spanish cause, another country being carved up by an aggressive neighbour.
6   Palafox was one of the few dynamic Spanish generals, and was soon to lead the determined resistance of the city of Saragossa against the French

GOYA'S VERSION OF THE EXECUTIONS

At last the Emperor's brother Joseph arrived from Naples, the Emperor having decided that he should swap his Neapolitan throne for that of Spain. The deputies of the Cortes had thought that they would find Ferdinand waiting for them in Bayonne. When they arrived from Spain, they were told that the Emperor had taken him into his protection. But in truth he had been sent to Valencay, which was no more than a polite way of imprisoning him. Instead of Ferdinand they found Joseph, whom the Emperor wished them to recognize as King of Spain, and to whom they were to swear an oath of loyalty. For this purpose a throne had been erected in the great chamber of the town hall, and the Cortes was invited to assemble there. When they had all gathered, King Joseph arrived and sat on the throne. The Emperor arrived just after him and waited in the vestibule. We ordered the doors to the chamber to be left ajar so he could hear the speech which Prince Infantado was to deliver to Joseph. The Prince spoke in French, very clearly and without an accent. In his speech he did not refer to any oath of loyalty, but spoke of the character and attributes of Joseph, and then said: "When the Spanish people are convinced of Your Excellency's worthiness, they will unite in their affection for you, and this will permit me to swear an oath of loyalty to you."

At this the Emperor flew into a rage, threw open the doors and rushed into the hall. He stopped in the space between the throne and the gathered deputies, and cursing roundly in French, shouted at Prince Infantado: "What did you come here for? If you had decided against accepting him you should have stayed away. But now you are here to acknowledge my brother as your king, address him as if he were your sovereign, and damn well swear allegiance!"

JOSEPH BONAPARTE AS KING OF SPAIN

The moment the Emperor burst into the room, his brother almost fell off the pedestal, so quickly did he leap up, and all the grandees, who by tradition were permitted to wear their hats in the presence of their King, immediately bared their heads. Infantado read out the pre-prepared oath, and they all repeated it with their hands raised.

The following day I was dining at the house of M. Champagny, and sat next to a Cortes deputy who had been summoned late from his province. He had only just arrived in Bayonne and had come straight to dinner with the minister. He knew nothing about the events of the previous day, and as his neighbor on the other side at table (the equerry Cavalotti) was too cautious to tell him anything, he directed his questions at me. I saw no reason to keep what had happened secret from him, as he would have found out from his colleagues. So in answer to his questions I told him that Ferdinand had been taken to Valencay, and that the Emperor had not acknowledged him as King and had forced his father Charles to abdicate in His favor. The deputy's face flushed red, he pushed away his food, stood up from the table and left the dinner. I later learned that he left Bayonne immediately. His name was Alawa. It was a pleasure for me to meet at least one Spanish nobleman with a sense of honor.

King Joseph left Bayonne for Madrid with all the deputies, but also with a strong escort of the Old Guard.

Napoleon's sister Caroline also came to Bayonne to join her husband Murat, who the Emperor had "promoted", as the French soldiers described it, to be King of Naples. She stayed a few weeks and livened up the evenings with the Empress. She had two ladies with her.

By now the Emperor must have realized that the Spanish would not submit to a change of dynasty, for he had already ordered several corps of the army to march into Spain. Regiments started passing through Bayonne. One of the first was Konopski's regiment of Polish lancers.[7] This was the old regiment from Dabrowski's Italian Legion, formed in Italy by Rozniecki from Galician prisoners and deserters from the Austrian army. It was a very fine and solid regiment, and all the officers and men were veterans. At the time Klicki was its Quartermaster. One morning before breakfast, the Emperor reviewed it in the park before the palace and ordered it through its paces. It performed its drill with such speed and accuracy that all the French officers declared there was no finer cavalry regiment in the army, not excluding the Guard. The Emperor ordered that its officers be entertained in the camp of the squadron of Polish guards. Captain Dziewanowski and his officers, among them Andrzej Niegolewski Wielkopolauie and Krzyzanowski, did the honors. Meanwhile, the other ranks of the Guard entertained the soldiers of the regiment under the trees. The Imperial household prepared everything. We had a grand time late into the night. The next day the regiment marched off to Spain, and three Polish infantry regiments arrived in Bayonne, from the old Italian Legion now renamed the Legion of the Vistula. They were very fine regiments, under General Grabinski, and later Chlopicki. The Emperor also passed them in review, and ordered the infantry of the Guard to entertain them. Officers looked after officers, and other ranks looked after their own.

A few days later two squadrons of German lancers from Berg arrived, whom Murat had dressed in Polish fashion, but there was a great difference in both their bearing and their drill, although their uniforms were far more elaborate.

During this time there also arrived in Bayonne, twelve regiments of Portuguese, which Junot, one of the Emperor's a.d.c.s who at that time was commanding a corps in Lisbon, had sent to France because he doubted their reliability. These regiments were understrength, as very many had deserted during the march through Spain. The ones that made it were in good condition, a small, gaunt, but very tough breed. Every day one regiment would come up to the chateau, march past the Emperor and set off for a garrison in southern France. They marched very quickly, even faster than the French. They wore white uniforms with different colored facings for each regiment. Two squadrons of Portuguese chasseurs à cheval also passed through, dressed in dark grey, one with green, and the other with blue collars. Apparently two entire regiments had left Portugal, but only a few hundred horses had reached Bayonne. Several regiments of French infantry and dragoons also passed through Bayonne, and the Emperor reviewed them all.

On 6 August the Emperor and Empress left for Paris through Pau, Agen, and Bordeaux. I was ordered to set off two days behind and bring reports from two generals, whose brigades were expected in Bayonne at any day. I caught up with the Emperor at Agen because he and

7 The 1st Vistula Lancers, later known also as the 7th Lancers of the French Army.

THE VISTULA LANCERS IN SPAIN

PRINCESS HORTENSE

the Empress had stayed the night in Pau and in Toulouse, while I had gone straight to Agen and arrived half an hour before him. An old artillery colonel was sitting in the orderly room with me. When the Emperor alighted from his carriage and entered the room and saw that the old man did not recognize him, he said:

"Don't you know me, colonel? Yet it was you who had me locked in the guard house!"

This colonel had been a captain in the artillery battery in which Napoleon had first served as a second lieutenant. So Napoleon now introduced himself as sublieutenant Bonaparte, and added that he was increasing the old man's pension.

The next day we went to Bordeaux, then to Rochefort, La Rochelle, Nantes, and then Paris, or rather straight to Saint Cloud. It so happened that I was the only orderly officer in attendance, so I was on continuous duty for a few weeks. I was given a room at Saint Cloud. Many visitors would come down to the palace, especially in the evening. Princess Hortense, the Empress's daughter, also lived there. She was not beautiful, but very nice. Shortly, three of my colleagues arrived, Tascher from Italy, Talhouet from St. Petersburg, and Eugene Montesquieu from Spain. We organized a duty roster of weekly shifts; Princess Hortense invited me to St. Leu, her summer palace a few hours from Paris, to a small reception on the occasion of the marriage of General Bertrand, one of the Emperor's a.d.c.s, to a relation of hers. I went with Tascher, who was the Princess's uncle.

A few days later, on 18 September, the Emperor sent me to see Caulaincourt, who was travelling from St. Petersburg to Erfurt with Tsar Alexander. I had to tell him the day and hour at which the Emperor would arrive in Erfurt to meet him. I reached Erfurt two days before Caulaincourt. The Tsar had stayed in Weimar where his sister lived. Only when Napoleon arrived at Erfurt did Alexander arrive, with a numerous entourage and his brother Constantine. The latter, when he saw that I was wearing nankeen cotton breeches instead of buckskin because of the heat, was very surprised, examined them closely and asked if we were allowed to wear them. A number of German princes and the King of Saxony also arrived. The festivities lasted for 12 days. They were lodged in houses around the city, but all of them dined with the Emperor at the Archbishop's palace, and their officers ate with us. Only English uniforms were missing, for otherwise they were there from every country in Europe, including even some Austrian generals. During the day all would go horseriding or take the Imperial carriages, and the Emperors' servants saw to everybody's needs. The Emperor had a French theater troupe brought from Paris, and they put on a show every night. Among others, they played "Britannia."

When the actor Talma said the lines;

"The friendship of a great man is a gift from the gods," Tsar Alexander (who, with the King of Saxony, was sitting either side of the Emperor at the front of the house) stood up from his place with great show, so that all could see him bow deeply to the Emperor.

After twelve days we returned to Paris. We were then ordered to send our remounts to Bayonne. But as the Emperor himself set off straight after and we with him, our remounts did not arrive in time and we each had to buy two new mounts in Bayonne and march after him into Spain.

Our first march took us to Irun. We only caught up with the Emperor at Burgos where he had halted, because the main Spanish army was drawn up on the plain before the city. As soon as the leading body of our army had arrived, that is one corps made up of three infantry divisions, a division of dragoons and half of the Guard, he deployed them, not in line but in battalion columns, with skirmishers in front. The skirmishers went into action, and the artillery must have fired about 500 rounds at the enemy. We could see confusion breaking out in the Spanish army. They tried only one charge. Some regiment which looked like black hussars, which I had never seen before, drew particular attention to themselves. Their attack failed, and was doomed from the start as they had begun to gallop at 1,000 paces and so were exhausted by the time they had covered half this distance. A regiment of French dragoons was sent out against them, but advanced only at a walk, and seeing that they would not reach it, it halted and sent out skirmishers, who were able to catch up with a dozen or so of the more poorly mounted hussars. Yet each of these, whether wounded or dismounted, fought on to the death, which proves these were valiant soldiers but they lacked experienced officers.

The same day the Emperor entered Burgos with part of his Guard. He sent a number of us back with various orders. I was sent to Marshal Lannes, who was in Catalonia outside Tudela. I arrived on 22 November.

He faced a Spanish corps that was said to far outnumber him, allegedly 40,000 men to Lannes' 18,000 or so. The Spanish corps, commanded by General Blake, of English family but born in Spain, stood in a strong position in the hills, which were perhaps too steep as artillery on such heights cannot fire downwards effectively. The Marshal was a little surprised by his order, which was to attack, but answered immediately, "As the Emperor wishes," and gave orders for 4 A.M. the following day. Before dawn, two infantry divisions set off up the hillside in four columns, with skirmishers out in front. The Spanish outposts half way up fired at them and retired to the summits, from which the artillery opened a heavy fire. For two hours the French columns did not stop, and their skirmishers duly reached the ridge line. An officer came down to the Marshal with the news that the whole Spanish corps was retiring and was everywhere in chaos. The Marshal had kept his cavalry brigade in the valley, not expecting such an easy time. He sent them off in quick pursuit, but it was already too late. Apart from two Spaniards captured by the skirmishers, no prisoners were taken.

The battles of Burgos and Tudela, if such two hour field maneuvers can be called battles, well justified Napoleon's proclamation to the army: "Soldiers! The Spanish are beaten; they could not stand up to your gaze!"

During my return journey from Lannes, I encountered Tascher in Tolosa, who was returning from Marshal Soult. We set off together to Mondragon with an escort of twenty hussars, for everywhere the Spaniards were shooting or ambushing solitary officers. Not far from Mondragon, where we were to change horses at the post house, he and I went on ahead

FRENCH INFANTRY PURSUING THE SPANISH IN THE MOUNTAINS

of our escort, for we had ordered its officer to slow his pace for the sake of his tired horses. After crossing a bridge over a mountain stream, Tascher and I caught up with a Spanish dispatch rider and we galloped along beside him. Then from the undergrowth some voices shouted: "Para! Para! [stop! stop!]" I think they must have been warning the post rider. At the same moment a dozen or so shots were fired and a bullet passed near me. But luckily the post rider, who had stopped, stood between me and the firers. As they clearly did not want

A Spanish Ambush

to kill the post rider, they shot wide and I was not hit. But Tascher's horse was wounded, and some grains of gun powder even struck him in the face, so close were they firing. But within a few seconds, the hussars, who were about 200 paces behind when they heard the shots, came dashing up to our rescue. By then the Spaniards were no longer to be seen; they had vanished into the undergrowth and back into the mountains.[8]

In Mondragon we received fresh horses and went on to Vittoria, Miranda, Burgos, Lerman, Aranda, and finally two days after the battle of Somosierra, about which we had been told on the way, we reached the battlefield itself. There were still several bodies of Polish light horsemen in the snow, which continued to cover the summit of Somosierra.

We stopped for half an hour in the village of Somosierra, where we found some severely wounded men who had not yet been transported. They told us about the charge by Dziewanowski's squadron, claiming all the officers and over half the men had been killed, while the survivors had taken the position and sixteen cannon. They assumed Lieutenant Niegolewski would also have died, as he had been badly wounded. While we were there, ambulances came to take the rest of the wounded to Madrid. From one of the surgeons I learned that as a reward for the charge of Somosierra the Emperor had promoted the whole Polish Guard Regiment to the Old Guard. This meant it had skipped the Middle Guard, as normally a regiment would go from the Young to Middle, and only after another act of heroism should it go to the Old Guard. This was a rise of two levels, so that a soldier in the Old Guard was senior to both a soldier and a corporal of the line, and so on. At that time the Old Guard comprised the Chasseurs à Cheval, the Grenadiers à Cheval, the Gendarmes of the Guard, and the Foot Grenadiers and Chasseurs. The Middle Guard was made up of the Dragoons and the Fusiliers. The Young Guard were the Tirailleurs and, until Somosierra, the Polish horse. So the Emperor, who witnessed the charge at Somosierra, must have thought it very fine to promote the regiment straight from Young to Old Guard, and he also ordered the whole Guard to present arms to the squadron as it passed by.

---

8 Tascher described this episode differently. When his horse fell wounded the Spanish grabbed him and were ready to carry him off. Chlapowski turned his horse around, charged at the man holding Tascher and fired his pistol into his face. The man let go and Tascher's life was saved.

SOMOSIERRA AFTER THE BATTLE

After a thirty minute break at Somosierra we went on our way, but they had no spare mounts at the post house. At every post house there were two gendarmes, who replaced the local Spanish postmasters who we could not trust. These gendarmes were the most experienced and wily soldiers, who could lay hands not only on two horses, but also on plenty of food. Of course, they knew each of us orderly officers and were aware we carried the Emperor's despatches, so even in a town or village which had been deserted and plundered, we could still rely on them to find us a meal. There were four squadrons of these so-called Gendarmes d'Elite, that is about 600 men.[9] Their commander was General Savary, an a.d.c. to the Emperor and later chief of police after Fouche.

After Buitrago and St. Augustin we reached Madrid and went straight to San Martin, a quarter of a mile from the city, where the Imperial Headquarters had been set up. San Martin, a castle with outbuildings, belongs to Prince Infantado. It stands in barren countryside, just like all the country around Madrid. We went back to the city. The next day I received an order to stay behind in Madrid for three days, where I was to report daily to Governor Belliard, then to follow and catch up with the Emperor on the road to Salamanca and give him all the news from Madrid. In those three days, although I must have walked all over the city, I got a good rest. I spent every evening and night at the Governor's residence. I met Niegolowski walking with a bandaged neck. He had already been nominated for the Legion of Honor.

9 In fact there was only one squadron of Gendarmes d'Elite in the Imperial Guard. Chlapowski is confusing some of these Guard Gendarmes with other gendarmes, which were deployed in Spain as well.

I set off by post horse on the evening of the third day. During the night I passed through Eskorial and Guadarame; the mountain was covered with snow and this sometimes reached the horse's chest, but the post rider knew the route well. By dawn I was at Villacastin, then passed through Arrevalo, Medina del Campo, Tordesillas, and finally at eleven at night I reached headquarters at Medina Rio Secco. The Emperor was not yet asleep; I found him in a white embroidered gown, green pantaloons and a little white and green night cap. Roustam the Mameluke was in the room, but he left on my arrival. The Emperor cross-examined me on all the gossip from Madrid. When any of us found himself in one place for several days, we had standing instructions to watch everything that happened, to see what troops arrived or departed, and to visit the military hospitals and receive reports from the doctors.

At headquarters I found my servants and my horses. The next day we moved to Valderas, turning left off the road to Salamanca. The British army under General Moore had marched from Salamanca toward Corunna, where a fleet of transports awaited it. The Emperor wanted to intercept his path through Valderas and Astorga. But several days of rain saved him, for the British were on a metalled road, and our road from Medina to Astorga was just a dirt track. There was snow, rain, and very cold temperatures, and the earth became such a mire that it took three days to march to Valderas instead of one. Horses and men sank deep into the mud. The older Grenadiers in the Guard said it reminded them of Pultusk. I was told that some soldiers who could not keep up with the column took their own lives for fear of falling into the hands of the Spanish guerillas, whose bands were roaming the country.

General Lefebvre Desnouettes had gone on ahead of the Emperor with the Chasseurs à Cheval of the Guard, and had used the road before the rain fell, so he had moved faster and advanced too far ahead of the army. He forded the River Esla by the town of Benevente. On the plain

GENERAL LEFEBVRE DESNOUETTES

before the town he was attacked by a whole division of British cavalry which had undoubtedly been told by spies that our army was still far behind. The General was forced to retreat rapidly over the river, and was himself captured with about 60 chasseurs on the river bank, as he had wanted to cross over last. The main army arrived on the banks of the Esla, which the rains had considerably swollen, to find the regiment in considerable confusion, for it had never met such misfortune before. But it was entirely the fault of their commanding officer, Lefebvre. Another regiment would undoubtedly been taken prisoner in its entirety; 600 men had faced 2,400 British cavalrymen. Even among those who got back across the river, many were wounded from pistol and carbine shots. Many displayed great bruises on their shoulders, backs and even some faces, and told us the English always struck with the flat of the blade instead of the point, for their swords were too broad and they did not know how to thrust their swords as the French cavalry did.

The Emperor sent a few of us off to right and left along the river bank with detachments of the Guard, in search of boats or wood for rafts. About 1,000 paces away, in a deserted village behind some undergrowth I found some boats, placed three voltigeurs on each, and rowed back to the Emperor.[10] On these we ferried some light infantry across to the evening bank, about a dozen to each boat. Fodoas, another orderly officer, took command of them and of a few squadrons which had crossed, some horses swimming, and some cavalry walking. A division of cavalry and some artillery arrived next on the river bank. The Emperor made the cavalry column close up to form a solid block without intervals, with officers in the ranks and everybody squeezed as tightly together as possible, and ordered it to march into the river above the ford, to form a living dam. The water level downstream of them fell, and the Emperor ordered the artillery to cross, which it did without even getting its ammunition wet. He followed right behind with the Staff. We arrived that night, wet and cold, at Benevente. This was in the last days of December.

That same night the Emperor sent me from Benavente to Marshal Bessieres, who had marched off a few hours before with a whole division to Astorga. The night was dark, the road was invisible, and there were no trees to mark its route. I led my horse by the reins and followed the tracks of the Marshal's cavalry, which had gone before me. I

CROSS OF THE LEGION OF HONOR

10 "The author does not record that the boats were on the far bank and that Chlapowski swam across to them and brought them back under enemy fire, for which he received the Officer's Cross." Comment by Count Tascher in the Polish edition.

VISTULA LANCERS IN SPAIN

caught up with the Marshal two miles down the road at Banoza, at about two in the morning. Within half an hour the whole division was in the saddle. We marched through Astorga and that day joined forces with the advance guard of Marshal Soult, who was coming up from Leon. It was commanded by General [Auguste] Colbert. Bessieres' division remained at Astorga and Colbert went on as far as Manzonales. A little beyond Carcavellos he encountered some Scottish light infantry in a good defensive position. He rode through the village with one platoon, for while he was waiting for his infantry to come up, he wanted to study the ground. The enemy fired a few shots, and a musket ball hit Colbert square on the forehead and he fell dead on the spot. As we withdrew from the village, my way was blocked in a narrow alley by a Scottish soldier; he grabbed my reins and thrust his bayonet at me, so I was obliged to run him through with my sword. This was the only time I ever killed an enemy; I always tried only to defend myself in combat. When I saw the Emperor again, at Banoza, I told him about the death of Colbert and he was most distressed.

The Emperor reached Astorga, but when he received a report from Marshal Soult, who was pursuing the English, he concluded he could not catch them before they reached Corunna. The English embarked on their ships, and being unable to take their horses but not wanting to let the enemy get them, cut the arteries on all the horses' forelegs.

From Astorga we went to Valladolid, from where the Emperor sent me off to the German princes, with the order to ready their forces immediately for war, as Austria had invaded Bavaria. I went with orderly officer Marboeuf (his father had been governor of Corsica and it was he who had sent the young Bonaparte to college in Brienne, so the Emperor liked the son very much; he was anyway a good man and soldier) through Southern France, Strasbourg, and Karlsruhe. Marboeuf went to Stuttgart and Munich, while I went to Darmstadt, Frankfurt, and Cassel, where Jerome was prince. Then I went to Dresden, where I did not find the King of Saxony, but had to follow him to Warsaw, where in fact I was going anyway. I reached Warsaw one morning after nineteen days and nights on the road. I had stopped nowhere, except for a few hours at each court, when in addition to handing over orders I had had to tell the Princes the news from Spain. I made the whole journey from Valladolid to Bayonne using post horses, and from Bayonne to Warsaw in my own light carriage. On the advice of an older, experienced traveller I had not eaten, but had only taken hot milk and bread three times a day at post houses, when I felt hungry. The weather was cold, and from Leipzig on the frost was so bad that I had to buy a fur.

In Warsaw I reported first thing to the French representative, Bourgoing, who lived in the Vienna hotel. He ordered his carriage to be ready for three o'clock, I changed my clothes, and together we went to the King of Saxony and Duke of Warsaw.[11] He received me politely. After receiving the Emperor's message, he asked me all about the events in Spain, then invited me to dinner.

That evening there was a ball at the Royal Palace. The King ended the ball with a polonaise at 10 P.M. Prince Poniatowski stayed for a little while longer, but when he left I also went off to rest.

It was marvelous to be back in Warsaw. I met nearly all of our senior officers. In truth our army was still organizing itself, but it already had a fine spirit. But there was an evident lack of experienced officers in all arms and there was a great difference between these new regiments and the Polish guard and Vistula Legion, with which I had recently been in Spain. As well as Colonel Krasinski, the entire staff of the Guard [the Polish Light Horse] were experienced officers and the regiment had soon become worthy of the older regiments of the Guard. The Vistula Legion still had officers from Dabrowski's Italian Legion and even Kniaziewicz's Legion of the Rhine. Nearly all the NCO's were older men, so training was steady, severe, and regular. It wasn't like that in the army of the Duchy of Warsaw. The infantry was admittedly first class, but the cavalry still needed a lot of work. Because the drill taught in the past had not been rapid enough, a new set of regulations was being produced. The artillery had only very few qualified officers, but the gunners were quite well trained. The whole army was learning and its excellent spirit, liveliness and cheerful confidence bade well for the future. In fact, only a small part of the army was stationed in the Duchy, as it provided the garrisons for Gdansk, Sczecin [Stettin], and Kistryn [Kustrin], and the pay sent to these garrisons did not come back to the country. The Duchy's finances also caused concern to the more serious citizens. All the money for equipping the army was flowing out of the country, for there were no factories at home to meet its needs. And the Duchy's sole income came from grain, which nobody could export at that time.[12]

Expenditure was beyond the capabilities of the country. There were too few properly trained administrators, as the Prussians had excluded Poles from this service. And the inflated number of bureaucrats absorbed too much revenue.

11 The Elector of Saxony had been created King of Saxony and Duke of Warsaw at the time Napoleon created the Duchy in 1807
12 Exports were disrupted because of the trade war between France and England.

I spent a week in Warsaw, collecting information about the state of the Austrian forces in Galicia. I was helped in this by Roman Soltyk, an officer in the new Polish Horse artillery, whom I had known from my time at the Ecole Polytechnique the previous year. His father lived at Szydlowiec, which at that time still belonged to Austria, so he knew, or rather was able to find out the whereabouts and numbers of Austrian forces. As I was under orders to pick up as much information as possible on this subject, I also enlisted the help of Heimcewicz, a relation on my mother's side, who gave me much information which the Emperor later found very useful.

Meanwhile, Marshal Davout had marched his corps straight to Silesia, and thence into Bavaria. He was instructed by the Emperor to place the Polish army under the command of one of its three generals of division, whom he was to choose himself. He decided to give command to Prince Joseph [Poniatowski]. The Saxon army, which had also been placed on a war footing, was ordered to be in Bavaria by the end of April.

When I got back to Paris, I found the Emperor in the Elysee Bourbon, preparing to leave for Germany. We all followed him to Strasbourg. Our servants and horses were to come to Strasbourg straight from Spain with the Guard, but as they were a long way behind, we were given 10,000 francs each to buy new horses. I bought one at a post house outside Stuttgart, and the second in Ingolstadt. I had my personal servant with me, and hired a groom from a post house in Wurtemburg. Our horses from Spain only reached us in Vienna. Until then the Emperor rode on horses belonging to the King of Wurtemburg.

NAPOLEON AT ECKMUHL, 1809

THE AUSTRIAN WAR OF 1809

The Emperor left Paris at 4 A.M. on 13 April. He was in Donauworth by 15 April, and we joined him there on the 16th. The next day the headquarters had reached Ingolstadt. On the way I noticed that the line of the River Lech had been recently fortified. It was clear that even though the Emperor certainly hoped to conduct a rapid advance, he was still securing his line of retreat.

On arrival at Ingolstadt, he toured the old fortifications and ordered new ones to be constructed outside them. As his forces were weaker than Austria's at that time, he was undoubtedly preparing for a defensive war. As we walked along the city walls, we could hear a heavy cannonade from the direction of Ratisbon. In the late afternoon, an officer arrived from Marshal Davout with the news that he was retiring before Archduke Charles' whole army; that he had left 3,000 foot in Ratisbon; that these had been forced to surrender, but that they had won him a day's march by holding up the enemy's advance; and finally that the Bavarian army had been beaten and was in rapid retreat.

At one in the morning [on 18 April] the Emperor called for me, and when I reported for duty he told me to sit at his table and copy from his campaign map onto a piece of tracing paper the route from Ingolstadt to Pfaffenhofen. Then he told me to take a squadron of the Wurtemburg Light Horse, which had been his escort while waiting for the Guard to arrive from Spain, and set off at once on reconnaissance toward Pfaffenhofen. He told me to move cautiously as the Austrians were in the town and would certainly be patrolling the Ingolstadt road. He added, however, that Marshal Massena was marching from Augsburg to Pfaffenhofen with orders to attack the Austrian left wing there, commanded by Archduke Ludwig, at 8 A.M. that same day. It is four german miles from Ingolstadt to Pfaffenhofen.

It was still dark at 4 A.M. when I took my place at the head of the squadron. One of the Emperor's a.d.c.s, General Mouton, then came up with an officer and six men of the Bavarian cuirassiers, saying the officer knew the region well, and could be useful. In truth, despite his youth, this man did prove a great help to me, for he came from this very area. When he assured me he knew all the side roads, I sent away the civilian guide who had been waiting to take us. We marched for a good two hours before it grew light, and then at the first inn I bought vodkas for the whole squadron. This was indeed a bargain, as for only a tiny sum, about two napoleons, I purchased, as they say, the goodwill of my soldiers. We set off on our way again, and I was soon told by the Bavarian that we had reached half way to Pfaffenhofen. The advanced guard of twelve Wurtemburgers, and officer and two Bavarians had just entered a pine wood, with the rest of us 500 paces behind, when we heard shots. I immediately deployed the squadron to left and right of the road, sent an order to the rearguard platoon 500 paces behind us to halt, and myself galloped up to join the advanced guard. When I got there I saw a group of French chasseurs à cheval who were firing on my Wurtemburgers. My men were shouting out, but the Frenchmen didn't understand them and had already wounded two men and knocked them off their horses, in the belief they were Austrians. For they could see helmets on my soldiers' heads, which they had never seen before in the French army, and moreover the white uniforms of the cuirassiers confused them, for they only ever pictured Austrians dressed in white, hence their nickname for Austrians which was, "soldats de creme." The French recognized my uniform,[1] and also their officer had arrived by then and

---

1 The uniform of an orderly officer to the Emperor, not a Polish uniform which would have been unfamiliar.

turned out to be a good friend of mine, young Lauriston, the son of the Emperor's a.d.c., who had been an Imperial page during the Spanish campaign. Massena was about to attack Pfaffenhofen, and had sent him with 80 chasseurs from the 20th regiment to scout in our direction. We organized ourselves as follows: I sent three platoons of Wurtembergers back to a good position we had passed along the way, ordering the quartermaster to send out pickets to the left to watch the Ratisbon-Pfaffenhofen road. I told him to feed the horses and prepare a fresh mount ready to take me back quickly to the Emperor. I left an officer and the fourth platoon at the spot where we had encountered the French chasseurs, and as there were a few huts in the distance to the right, I permitted this man to send a detail there in search of food for men and horses. I gave him four napoleons so he would not take anything without payment, for whereas it is damaging for soldiers to steal food on campaign, it is all the more so if soldiers on reconnaissance do it, as the inhabitants run away from their villages, confusion spreads throughout the countryside, and it becomes harder still to feed the main army. The Imperial treasury always used to reimburse me and my fellow officers for such expenditure. I advised this officer also to place two pickets with good fields of view.

Lauriston gave me a fresh horse and one of his chasseurs as guide, who already knew the road to Pfaffenhofen, having just come from there. I arrived in a short time, just as Marshal Massena's infantry reached the town. His cavalry had already passed through Pfaffenhofen and were on its far side. The Austrians had not defended the town at all; in truth, this place is not well suited to defense. They had retired on Landshut, where Archduke Louis had his headquarters.

I knew the Emperor was waiting anxiously in Ingolstadt for news of Massena's arrival at Pfaffenhofen, so I asked the Marshal for a good horse which I could ride into the ground. He gave me an a.d.c.'s horse and an officer of his staff to accompany me, but this man could not keep up with me, for within an hour I had reached my first platoon where a good Wurtemburg horse awaited me. From there I raced like the wind to my other three platoons, where the quartermaster waited. He had been so gracious as to make ready the better of his own two horses for me to use. In this way, having taken four hours to travel from Ingolstadt to Pfaffenhofen, I needed only two hours for my return journey. When I reported to the Emperor his first words were, "What did you encounter on the road which stopped you getting through?"

He was very content to learn that Massena's corps was already at Pfaffenhofen. It was 10 A.M. on 18 April. He sent me off to rest, but after two hours I had to hurry after him again, for on receipt of the news about Massena the Emperor had set off to join the Bavarian army. He placed this army under the command of General Lefebvre, because under the Bavarian Crown Prince Ludwig, it had been beaten by the Austrians. On arrival at the Bavarian camp the Emperor gathered all its officers together in a ring. He went into the circle with the Prince and his generals (among them Wrede and Roy) and asked the Prince to translate what he said into german. We could not hear what he said, as the circle was too broad and we were outside it. It was even harder because Prince Ludwig had a pronounced stammer. We later learned that the Emperor had told them he had come to free their country from the Austrian invaders and that he would lead them as far as Vienna, but that they would have to fight better. Straight after this speech he ordered the whole army to stand to arms, form column and march, because we could already hear small arms and occasional cannon fire in the distance, about half a mile, or perhaps a mile in front of Ratisbon.

FRENCH CUIRASSIERS ADVANCING ON AUSTRIANS

The Emperor and his staff set off at a gallop after the Bavarian cavalry, which we caught up with after half an hour. They numbered six regiments and some horse artillery, but their demoralization was obvious. Their artillery was firing from very long ranges at the Austrian horse,[2] which was advancing boldly toward the Bavarians in two columns with flankers, mostly ulans, to left and right. This encounter took place between Tann and Abensberg. But away to the left of the Ingolstadt-Ratisbon road there shortly appeared a division of French infantry and a brigade of French cuirassiers, which put a new slant on things. As soon as the Austrian cavalry saw the cuirassiers, they drew in their flankers and began to retire behind their infantry. The cuirassier regiments deployed at a trot. The ground did not favor them, as it was covered in bushes, so when they began their advance they appeared to be attacking in a skirmish formation, not in line. Even so, they fell upon the Austrian foot so suddenly that it was taken by surprise, and instead of forming square to cover its own cavalry to its rear, it was thrown into such complete confusion that even the Bavarian horse took heart at this bold assault and joined in the pursuit.

The cuirassiers and Bavarians began leading prisoners back past the Emperor. Most of them were infantrymen. The Emperor dismounted in the open field and ordered a fire to be lit, as it was already dusk. Davout's second division arrived and marched in column right by the Emperor. The soldiers, who had thought him still to be in Spain, let out such cheers when they recognized him as I had never heard before. At that same moment a dozen or so cuirassiers passed by on his other side with a column of about 5,000 prisoners, including many

---

2   A clear sign of nervousness. Seasoned or confident gunners would not waste ammunition at extreme range, but would unlimber close enough to the enemy to do him damage. The Bavarians were obviously not keen to get to grips.

AUSTRIAN STAFF OFFICERS

officers, who had been captured late in the day. A colonel of their general staff had also been captured, and was brought before the Emperor. The Emperor told him to sit by him and started asking him about the positions and strengths of the Austrian corps. The Austrian started to answer, then stopped and said one could not demand that an officer of the staff give such information to the enemy.

"Do not worry, Sir," said the Emperor, "I know everything anyway," and he described quickly and accurately the locations of all the corps and which regiments were serving in them. The Austrian, astonished that his interlocutor was so well informed of such details, said: "With whom do I have the honor [of speaking]?" At this the Emperor inclined himself forward, touched his hat and replied, "Monsieur Bonaparte." Throughout this interview the French infantry continued to cheer as it marched by. It was a beautiful sight: on one side the French infantry, full of confidence, striding forward, and elated to see their Emperor, and on the other a column of prisoners, some of whom, so at least it seemed to us, were also cheering him.

By eleven o'clock, the night was very dark and the Emperor mounted his horse and went to the closest village, Rohr, where quarters had been made ready. Beside the hut prepared for him, there was a one room hut for the rest of us. After a very short supper, which made do as lunch and dinner, we lay down on good straw mattresses prepared by the palace farrier. But we had been warned at supper that we would have only two hours to rest, and at 3 A.M. [on 19 April] the Emperor and his whole staff were mounted and on the road to Landshut.

Archduke Charles commanded the main Austrian army, but it was generally known that the Imperial Council in Vienna kept sending him instructions. So his army stood immobile in obedience to Vienna's wishes, as if it were in no danger of an enemy attack. His right wing under Marshal Bellegarde was north of the Danube between Ratisbon and Amberg; the center

56

ARCHDUKE CHARLES

under Archduke Charles was south of the Danube and Ratisbon, and the left wing under Archduke Ludwig was at Landshut. These three corps together were as much as 160,000 men strong. Besides this army, Austria had 60,000 men in Italy, 45,000 in Galicia and an independent corps on the Saxon border.

The Emperor had no more than 100,000 men under arms, but after linking up with Massena, he had his troops all together and, as we shall see, outnumbered the enemy at every point he attacked.

From 3 A.M. to 8 A.M. we covered four miles, passing columns of infantry and cavalry, which had been marching all night on either side of the road with artillery moving down the middle. The Emperor left the forest and entered the plain before Landshut just as Massena was attacking Archduke Ludwig's camp.

The Emperor's column arrived on the right of the Austrian position. He straight away ordered the cuirassier division to deploy, told the front regiment to charge the enemy infantry which was turning to face us, and ordered the artillery to open fire without delay. The infantry, which had kept up with the cavalry all night, emerged from the forest, deployed into columns, and set off at the double after the cuirassiers, its drummers beating the charge.

Archduke Ludwig's whole command began to retreat through Landshut. We had a clear view of them as their cavalry trotted over the bridge across the river Izar, with their infantry following right behind. On the far side of the bridge the main road into the town sloped uphill so that we could clearly see it jam-packed with troops of all arms. On our side of the bridge the cuirassiers and Massena's light horse captured a few thousand prisoners. But when our cavalry set foot on the bridge they were stopped by canister fire from up the road, and heavy small arms fire from the surrounding houses. A column of our infantry, ignoring the bullets, then crossed the bridge, charged into the town, and rounded up a good many more Austrians. The Emperor's forces were far stronger here than the Archduke Ludwig's. From his position in the town, the Archduke must have seen the French columns converging on his camp from two directions. All his men would also have been able to see that our ring of troops would surround their position. This sight must surely have had an effect on Austrian morale, and convinced them that the battle was lost before it even started. This must have explained why the engagement was so short. It had begun at 8 a.m., we were in the town at eleven and eating lunch by 12:30.

At 1 P.M. [on 19 April] the Emperor called for me and sent me to Marshal Davout, whom he had left with two divisions of infantry facing the whole army of Archduke Charles, which must have been at least 60,000 strong. I copied out my route from the Emperor's detailed map

FRENCH CAVALRY AND INFANTRY AT THE DOUBLE

and set off right away. Instead of following the main highway which curved off to the right, I rode straight for Eckmuhl, where the Emperor told me I would find the Marshal. I was instructed to tell him that by midnight, the Emperor and the whole army would arrive at Eckmuhl on the Ratisbon road.

Before he sent me off, the Emperor said to me: "At 8 this morning I sent one of Marshal Davout's own aides de camp back to him. He was a fellow countryman of yours, but I reckoned from the look of him that he would not get there very quickly. If he does arrive before you, you should anyway tell the Marshal about the capture of Landshut and retreat of Archduke Ludwig."

At the first village, three quarters of a mile from Landshut, I went to the local mayor to demand a guide to show me the quickest way to Eckmuhl. The mayor was standing in his window, and I was talking to him from horseback. He pointed to an officer sleeping on straw in the room behind him and said he also had requested a guide, but not until 4 P.M. I entered the room and woke the sleeping man. I recognized him a F.P., the very man whom the Emperor had despatched that morning to Marshal Davout. I urged him to follow me, but he was undressed and said he must eat first, as he had ridden all night. So when the guide appeared on his horse outside the house, I went on my way and left F.P. to it. The Emperor had judged his bearing well. I don't think F.P. ever had a desire to be a soldier. Advancing in years, married and with children, he had joined Davout's staff in Warsaw out of a sense of patriotism. I recount this anecdote here only to show how the Emperor could gage people with one glance, and at least assess their military abilities. Such an eye is one of the attributes of a good commander-in-chief.

My guide was well mounted and I reached the Marshal at 5 P.M. I was spurred on by the sound of gunfire, which I first heard an hour before I reached my destination, but which had stopped completely by the time I had arrived. I found the Marshal standing in front of his batteries on a hill, over looking Eckmuhl and the whole Austrian army, which had been attacking him since morning, but had failed to dislodge his two infantry divisions from the strong position he had selected. He told me that every time he saw enemy infantry columns approaching the foot of the hill, he had sent all the artillery horses to the rear, to show the soldiers there could be no retreat. Enemy columns had three times advanced up the hillside, and every time the Marshal had let them get within close range, then stopped them in their tracks with canister and small arms fire. The last time, after firing with all his artillery, he had led his first line of infantry in a bayonet charge. The Austrians had broken and mounted no more attacks thereafter. A hundred paces from the battery and all the way down to the foot of the hill, the ground was littered with dead Austrians. For this fine defense Davout was to be given the title Prince of Eckmuhl.

When the Emperor's infantry had entered Landshut, he had ordered his cavalry, a light division and a cuirassier division, not to enter the town but immediately to take the Ratisbon road. Behind them followed the greater part of his artillery and infantry. So an hour after my arrival with Davout, that is at about 6 p.m., we noticed that the Austrian army was beginning to retire toward Ratisbon. From time to time we also heard artillery shots coming from the Landshut road. Archduke Charles must have had detachments out on the Landshut-Eckmuhl road, which had encountered the French cavalry advancing from Landshut. He must also have learnt about the defeat of his brother Ludwig, and so have concluded that the Emperor was turning his left flank with the main French army. So he must have started his retreat along the road to Ratisbon to join up with Marshal Bellegarde.

By about 8 P.M. the firing had drawn so close that we could see the flashes in the cannons' mouths and I rode into Eckmuhl (my horse had been fed by the Marshal's staff). There I found the very cuirassiers who had left Landshut at eleven that morning. Together with the rest of the army with the Emperor, they had been on the march for twenty four hours non-stop. At eleven o'clock the previous night they had left Abensberg, at 8 A.M. were at Landshut and at eleven o'clock at night had passed through Eckmuhl and were only two miles from Ratisbon. Undoubtedly many horses were exhausted, but those that survived the journey made such an impression with their arrival that the Austrian generals lost their senses. The infantry marched right behind the cavalry and if anything did not seem as tired as them.

By midnight [on 19 April] the Emperor arrived at Ergolzbach, where we spent the rest of the night, and at 6 A.M. [on 20 April] we set off toward Ratisbon, The Emperor rode right behind the leading regiment of chasseurs à cheval. By 8 A.M. we could see the towers of Ratisbon in the distance. The Austrians had left pockets of infantry in all the villages. As we only had cavalry with us, we could not march through these villages, so had to ride around them across the fields. To our front we could see only skirmishers, hussars, and Archduke Charles' Ulans with their distinctive red headgear. When the Austrian infantry saw we were detouring past them, they retreated hastily after their cavalry. Half a mile from Ratisbon, we reached an area of open high ground overlooking the town in the valley. Below us, we saw the last proper village before Ratisbon, and behind it a mass of enemy cavalry, with lancers in the front line. The Emperor mounted a hillock close to the village, from whose gardens a dozen or so shots were fired in our direction. A squadron of line chasseurs were riding close behind the Emperor (for the Guard was still far to the rear).[3] The Emperor ordered me to take this squadron and clear the village. The chasseurs advanced rapidly, ignoring the enemy fire, dismounted and closed with the enemy. A few hundred Austrians surrendered. They were from the Archduke Charles' infantry regiment, and among them was an officer, called Ignacy Ledochowski. When the chasseurs returned with the prisoners, the Emperor spotted Ledochowski, walking at their head and making a striking impression with his excessively youthful face, his beautiful white uniform with its bright blue collar, and his gilded helmet towering over those of his men. The Emperor summoned him over and asked his name. On learning that he was a Pole from Galicia, he said to him: "And why are you serving the invaders of your country?"

Having said that, he whipped his horse and set off again at a gallop. Ledochowski was standing so close that the end of the Emperor's whip knocked his helmet, and thinking the Emperor had deliberately struck him, he was so mortified that he nearly wept with grief. He would not have been so upset if he had known, as we did, that the Emperor never used his spurs or knees to make his horse gallop, but always applied his whip. I could not persuade him that the Emperor had not intended to hit him, nor would dream of doing so.

The cuirassier division arrived, with the brigade of Carabiniers at its head. The Emperor deployed it straight away, for he saw that the Austrian cavalry, in columns in front of Ratisbon, had begun to advance toward us. Soon an ulan regiment in six squadrons trotted up to within 200 paces of the Carabiniers and launched a charge at full tilt. It reached their line, but could not break it, as the second regiment of Carabiniers was right behind the first, and behind it the rest of the cuirassier division. I saw a great many Carabiniers with lance wounds, but a dozen or so ulans had also fallen. Among our prisoners was a warrant officer, a fine looking man. A Carabinier had cut him to the bone from his ear to his eye, and his blood flowed over his green uniform and onto the ground. Yet his headdress had not fallen off, and was still perched loftily on his head. The Emperor, learning the Austrian Ulans were Poles, bade me ask this man if he did not know that the Emperor wished to take Poland from those who had dismembered it and give it back to us. He answered bravely:"I do know this, and if a Polish officer had approached our regiment we would have all followed him. But when we are ordered to charge we have to get on and do it, so nobody can say Poles are bad fighters."

After this charge, the whole Austrian cavalry retreated behind Ratisbon. Maybe the charge by the ulans had been intended to cover this withdrawal. The Emperor approached closer to the town, stood on some high ground with a good field of vision and looked through his telescope. There were still Austrian skirmishers in the gardens on the outskirts, firing in our direction. A bullet hit the Emperor in the foot. He got off his horse, his boot was removed and Iwan, his private surgeon, bandaged his toe which had been badly bruised by the bullet, and cut a hole in the boot so it would not be too tight.* The Emperor got right back on his horse and returned at a gallop to the army. He had ordered that it form up by regiments and that the officers of each be told to select the most courageous from among their number. The officers duly stood at the head of each regiment and presented their nominees to the Emperor,

3   It was usual for the Emperor to be escorted by a duty squadron when in the field. This task was undertaken by the Guard regiments in rotation. At this stage of the campaign however, the Guard was still on its way from Spain, so line cavalry and even German cavalry regiments had the honor.
*   This is the scene depicted on the cover.

and the Emperor made each a baron and awarded him a pension. He also made me and some other officiers d'ordonnance barons, and gave us each a pension of 4,000 francs.

Ratisbon has old defenses, on which the Austrian infantry were assembled. Hardly had our batteries unlimbered and fired a dozen or so volleys than our infantry burst into the city and captured several thousand Austrians. Their main army was already on the far bank of the Danube, but they had retreated so hastily that the bridge had not been destroyed, or perhaps Archduke Charles had not ordered its destruction, knowing that the Danube is broad here and it would be easy for us to make another bridge. That same evening Davout's Corps crossed the bridge and marched after the Austrians. The Emperor entered Ratisbon, and we spent the whole of 21 April there, for the army needed a rest after three days and nights of continuous advancing. We had had to leave many exhausted men along the way.

FRENCH ENGINEERS BUILDING BRIDGE

After the rest day we returned to Landshut. Marshal Lannes's Corps had the previous day pursued the remnants of Archduke Ludwig's forces, and captured an entire pontoon train, which the prisoners informed us had been intended for crossing the Rhine.

We crossed the rivers Isar and Inn at Braunau and reached Wels by 3 May. The Austrians had burnt the wooden bridge across the Danube at Wels. I was standing on the riverbank when General Bertrand himself supervised the building of a new one and I was amazed by the speed with which it was laid, even in the absence of pontoons (the French army had no pontoon train in this war, and the equipment captured from Archduke Ludwig had not been brought up). Laying bridges in an area with many wooden buildings is very easy. First, a handful of sappers crossed the river in a little boat and stretched a rope from bank to bank. Then they tied boats and logs side by side along this line. Boats which had higher sides than the rest were weighed down with rubble and stone, until they were all level in the water. Right on top were placed the planks on which to walk. When they ran out of boats, they made rafts from wood torn from local buildings. Within six hours there stood a bridge which cavalry, artillery, and, of course, infantry began to cross.

The Emperor crossed the bridge soon after the first units of the army, and followed a minor road to Ebensburg, which we reached during the night of 4 May. The Austrian defense of the town had been fierce. A great many French corpses lay in front of and on the bridge leading to the city gate. But the enemy had not succeeded in blowing up the bridge. After a fierce struggle the French had broken into the town and ran amok among the Austrians, leaving many corpses around the streets. Claparede's division was made up of Corsican regiments who, having lost many men before taking the town, exacted a terrible revenge afterwards.

The Emperor refused to enter the town until the following morning. I think even

Marshal Massena

he was disturbed by the sight of this carnage. A shelter was made for him from saddle clothes, and the rest of us just lay down on the ground. I was lying by a ditch, and was falling off to sleep when I heard a groan right behind my head and the words in Polish, "Jesus, Marya, Josef!" I jumped up and saw an Austrian soldier, lying stretched out nearby, but he would say nothing more. He was still breathing, but had lost consciousness. War is always filled with horrors, but we Poles have to suffer some of the worst, for everywhere we are forced to fight our own flesh and blood.

After passing through Ebensberg, the Emperor retraced his steps and moved his headquarters to Enns, two miles from there.

Throughout the Austrian retreats from Ratisbon and Landshut there had been ulans in their rearguard. The Emperor ordered a squadron of Polish Guard cavalry to advance by forced marches to join the main army. This squadron, under Lieutenant Colonel Lubienski, arrived while we were at Enns. He was sent off to our advanced guard with orders to send a handful of cavalrymen to every unit and outpost in the picket line. Whenever the Austrian ulans encountered our men, they would come over to us in ones or twos, and sometimes several together. But after a few days the Austrians withdrew the ulan regiment and gave the job of rearguard to some hussars.

Marshal Massena had marched from Ratisbon to Scharding on the Danube. He must have ordered Claparede to attack Ebensberg because he could not have known that the Emperor have crossed the river at Wels and was already advancing from the other side. His communications with the Emperor must have been inadequate, for otherwise he would not have attacked on 4 May, knowing that the Emperor would arrive with a corps on the far bank that evening. The Austrians would have either retired, or have been captured.[4]

The enemy had destroyed the bridge at Enns, but by the 5th we had already rebuilt it. It is never worth destroying bridges in your own country, because it takes no time for an advancing army to rebuild them, especially the French, as their engineers are so efficient and experienced that during periods of rest, which armies just like people have to have, they can build a new bridge easily, but with no little hardship for the inhabitants, whose houses have to be demolished in the process.

The Emperor, who had still been on the road from Wels to Ebensberg when he heard of the latter's capture, had straight away sent the order back to Marshal Lannes not to follow him, but to march from Wels to Steyer. This corps joined up with us at Amstetten, where our cavalry conducted a number of charges against the Austrian horse. I was with Colonel Aldobrandini, whom I knew well. He had a regiment of cuirassiers which after one charge got into a melee with some Hungarian hussars. I was surprised to see when the Hungarians retreated that far more of their bodies were lying dead than French. The main reason for this was that the Hungarians slashed with their sabers, while the French thrust. I don't think one cuirassier died of a saber cut, but a few dozen were shot by artillery fire. About a hundred of the Hungarians were taken prisoner.[5]

On 8 May, the main headquarters was at Molk, in a large, beautifully situated, Benedictine monastery. On the 9th we were at St. Polten, from whence the Emperor sent me that evening with a squadron of chasseurs à cheval and instructions to march toward Vienna. I was to take only side roads to the right of the main highway, and was to find anybody who had been in the city that day, or who had reliable news from the capital. I passed through six pretty little villages in all. The inhabitants were sleeping everywhere except in one, where we saw lights in a few houses and white Austrian uniforms. But as soon as the first chasseurs appeared, the lights went out and everything fell silent. They must have been marauders, who decided to hide from us. I continued on my mission, although the captain of chasseurs wanted to take these Austrians, but I denied him this pleasure as it would have held me up and distracted me from my task. I told him we could seek them out on our way back. From then on I ordered the officer commanding the advance guard, consisting of twelve men, to wake up the occupants of one house in every village we passed, so that when I arrived with the main body 200 paces behind, I would not have to wait too long and could talk to these occupants while the squadron filed past. Then, when the rearguard approached, I would catch up to the squadron with my aide and my trumpeter. Only in the sixth village was I able to find a priest, who had been in Vienna the previous day. He told me Archduke Maximilian was in command in Vienna with twelve battalions of infantry. He did not know which direction the Archduke Ludwig had retreated (in fact, the Emperor already knew that Ludwig had crossed the Danube at Krems, no doubt in order to link up with Archduke Charles).

I returned to St. Polten at about 9 A.M. on 10 May and the squadron got back two hours later.

---

4 Chlapowski is mulling over why the battle of Ebensburg had to take place at all.. If Massena had known Napoleon was coming, he need not have caused such bloodshed.

5 It is interesting that Chlapowski should be surprised. Received 20th century wisdom is that heavy cavalry would always have the edge over lighter cavalry such as hussars. He attributes the disparity in losses to weapon handling. Perhaps when it came to a confused melee (as opposed to a formed charge) swordsmanship counted more than the weight of horse and rider.

I changed horses in St. Polten, then set off after the Emperor, who had covered the four miles to Schoenbrunn almost at a gallop and then continued until he reached the outer defences surrounding the outskirts of Vienna. Here I saw a sight which I would not have believed had I not seen it with my own eyes and heard with my own ears. Even then I found it hard to believe. The city walls were not crowded, but there were still a good many well-to-do inhabitants on the ramparts. The Emperor rode right up the glacis, so only a ditch 10 meters wide separated him from these people. When they recognized him, from the last time he had been there in 1805, they all took off their hats, which I supposed could be expected, and then began cheering, which seemed unnecessary and less fitting to me. I could only explain such behavior by, on the one hand, the indifference to world events of the people of large cities, especially the Viennese, and on the other hand by the devotion which a man like the Emperor inspired in all around him. When I expressed my surprise to some French officers, they assured me that they had seen and heard exactly the same thing at the Brandenburg Gate in Berlin in 1806.

THE CITY WAS SET ON FIRE IN A FEW PLACES

The Emperor left the highway and rode clockwise around the perimeter of the defenses. He rode briskly along for about thirty minutes until he reached a corner, and from time to time he raised his hat in response to the cheering, just as if he were riding around Paris. He had ordered the squadron which accompanied him from St. Polten to remain in the rear, and only an escort of twenty five men followed him, 200 paces behind. When he reached the angle in the defenses he turned his horse around and rode slowly back to Schoenbrunn. He turned to me and told me to hurry back to the palace to lie down, saying "A bed will already be made up for you there. You've spent so many nights on horseback, it's time you had a comfortable rest courtesy of the Emperor Francis. You'll be back in the saddle tomorrow."

As I rode to the castle at Schoenbrunn, I passed the heads of the columns of Oudinot's combined grenadiers and voltigeurs, who were already done up in full dress, with plumes in the headgear ready for the triumphant entry into Vienna. In the palace I found the Imperial

Eugene Beauharnais, Viceroy Of Italy

household. One of them showed me to some rooms upstairs which had been allocated to us, in each of which were two beds.

The Emperor's manservant brought me a big pineapple, of which I was told there were many in the gardens, a bottle of wine, some bread and some ham. I undressed and slept wonderfully.

My colleague Talhouet was put in the same room as me. At 7 P.M. he woke me for dinner, but he did not return to sleep there that night as the Emperor had sent him to Oudinot, who had reported that he had passed through the outskirts of Vienna without mishap, but that the Austrians had fired cannon at him from the walls of the main city, which they seemed determined to defend. So the Emperor ordered earthworks to be dug during the night under the noses of the Hungarian guards, and sent a battery of siege howitzers to be deployed there. The city was set on fire in a few places, but as he did not wish to turn it into an inferno, the next day he sent Molitor's division on a detour around right of the city to Ebersdorf. On the 14th the Emperor himself arrived there and sent Talhouet with 200 voltigeurs across the Danube on boats to the crossroads of Pratern. From there, Pourtales, who was Berthier's a.d.c., then swam with a dozen or so voltigeurs across the stretch of the Danube separating Pratern from Vienna. This all happened as night was falling. Archduke Maximilian must have thought the whole French army was crossing over into the city, for early next morning he evacuated Vienna. Our army entered the city on the 15th, and the Emperor returned to Schoenbrunn.

That day the Emperor heard the news that the Austrian General Chasteller was approaching from Styria and Hungary, with a division of reservists and landwehr. So he sent a squadron of Polish Guard horse under Lieutenant Colonel Lubienski to Neustadt with orders to find a position in the locality from which, with the help of informers and patrols, they could follow all Chasteller's movements. Lubienski was instructed to compile reports daily. I was ordered to collect them, and to establish whether Chasteller was advancing or anything significant had occurred.

On 18 May I received a report that Chasteller was withdrawing to link up with Archduke John, who was retreating from Lombardy before the advance of the Viceroy of Italy, Eugene Beauharnais, from Udina.

It may seem strange that the Emperor should send out only one squadron to cover an area which a whole Austrian division was reported to occupy, but all he wanted was information about Chasteller's movements. For this task, he could rely totally on Lt. Colonel Lubienski, whose ability was highly regarded.

The Emperor always liked to keep all his strength together in one place, especially when he expected a major engagement. He knew well that when you win the main battle, secondary factors lose their importance. In this case he could safely assume that Chasteller would not approach with only one division, when up to 80,000 Frenchmen were in the vicinity of Vienna and especially when the Guard, just arrived from Spain, were setting up camp to the south of the city. The whole Grand Army numbered more than 80,000, but Davout's corps was still to the rear observing Archduke Charles across the Danube. The Saxons under Bernadotte were still traipsing across north Bavaria, and the Bavarians were with Lefebvre in the Tyrol, where a rebellion had broken out. So in all there were no more than 80,000 men around Vienna, and as many again in the various other corps elsewhere in Europe.

The Emperor also did not want to frighten Chasteller by sending superior numbers against him, as he believed that the Austrian was wasting his time where he was. The Emperor preferred him to stay there, where he could achieve nothing, than to go off to join Archduke John, who thus reinforced could all the more effectively slow up the advance of the Army of Italy.

The Emperor wanted to link up with the Army of Italy as soon as possible, because although Archduke John's army was also approaching the main area of operations, it had further to go through Hungary and Moravia to join up with Archduke Charles than did the Viceroy of Italy, whose march from Udina toward Hungary was bringing him closer to the Emperor's main army.

On 18 May, the Emperor sent me to Ebersdorf to inspect the pontoon train. I found it to be in good condition and gave a favorable report. When the Emperor arrived in the evening, he sent two companies of voltigeurs across to the island of Lobau. On 19 May, Molitor's entire division crossed over. Soon a bridge was also laid across the second channel of the Danube so by the 20th three corps were already on the island.[6]

That day two bridges were thrown across the last channel of the Danube, under the protection of a battery of heavy artillery that had been dug into the near bank. This channel is narrower than the first. At about 4 o'clock in the afternoon General Lasalles' entire light cavalry division crossed over, and me with it. As we emerged from the trees which lined on the river bank, Austrian howitzers began firing shells at us, but they did not hamper the division as it deployed its five regiments in two lines on the plain behind Aspern and Esling. At about 7 p.m., after a fierce cannonade, the Austrians launched a ferocious cavalry attack on us. Enemy hussars made a vigorous frontal attack on Piret's first brigade (which was made up of the 8th Hussars and 16th Chasseurs à Cheval), while a regiment of ulans attacked it from the left flank. The enemy hussars had reached only 200 to 250 paces away from us, and were cantering along with shouts and hurrahs, when General Lasalle began to advance at a walk, then trot, and finally at a gallop so he hit the hussars at full tilt. A regiment of the second line wheeled to the left to engage the ulan regiment. The opposing sides got as mixed up together as shredded cabbage. It was also getting dark by then. The confusion, the din, and the uproar lasted an hour. The cannons had long since ceased firing.

Finally, the Austrian horse disengaged, and Lasalles' division again reformed in two lines, but a few hundred paces behind the position it had held before the charge. So, as they say, it

---

6 The Danube has several channels at this stage of the river.

66

FRENCH CHASSEURS FIGHTING AUSTRIAN CAVALRY AT ASPERN

had lost ground. Afterwards, the Austrian guns fired a dozen or so round into the darkness. I don't know where the shots were landing; they didn't even fly over our heads.

The night was clear. Generals Lasalle and Piret went forward to oversee the placement of out posts and sentries. There were fewer bodies on the ground than you might expect after such a ding-dong fight, but of those we saw, there must have been almost twice as many enemy as French (although nobody actually counted them). This imbalance must have come from the fact that the Hungarians brandish their sabers around a great deal, whereas the French thrust with the point. And although the Hungarian on his lighter horse can easily dance out of the way of the Frenchman on his less maneuverable mount, the latter can gage the Hungarian's angle of attack, parry the enemy's cut and then puncture his chest with the point of his nearly straight sword. The Hungarians don't slash with the side of the blade like the English do, but when they attempt to strike with the tip of their curved sabers they always do so in a rush or as they turn their horses aside, so they lunge without much idea of where they will hit.

The enemy had charged us three or four times during this engagement. Some of them would break into our ranks, many passed right through and circled back to regain their lines, and after every charge they ended in complete disorganization. The French, on the other hand, although they also lost formation after a charge, kept together far more and every time were quicker to regain order. I suppose after all that, besides their superior swordsmanship, they had more battle-hardened troops and officers than the Austrians.

From what I have said about the difference between the French on heavier, and the Austrians on lighter, horses, the reader should not conclude that heavier horses are better for light cavalry. Not in the least. For if you could put experienced troopers on light horses, give them still more experienced officers and train them to use their swords for thrusting rather than cutting, you will have the best light cavalry of all. An experienced trooper knows what he's about, and when order has to be maintained in the line, he is able to control his lively mount, whereas he can give it its head when skirmishing or in an individual combat. I am describing only the circumstances particular to that campaign, which were that although the Hungarians drove home their attacks with determination, they were harder to reform into some sort of order. The French, on the other hand, knew that their own horses lacked the Austrians' speed and endurance, and would launch their attacks from closer range and so retained formation right to the end of the charge, and regained it more quickly afterwards. The Hungarians, waving their sabers above their heads , or skirting around enemy horsemen, often ended up striking thin air. Even when they struck home, the best they achieved was a bad wound. The French never swung their swords about, and were able to defend against enemy cuts, and, having parried, with one thrust could strike an often mortal blow. I, too, was wounded on the leg above the ankle by a Hungarian that day, but his sword twisted in his hand and the wound was not deep. But it was quite a blow and I felt it for many years.[7]

When everything had quietened down I returned to the Emperor, whom I found under a shelter of branches by the bridge across the last stretch of the Danube. I reported that General Lasalle occupied a position on the plain between Aspern and Esling. That same night the Emperor sent infantry and artillery across to occupy and fortify these villages. Throughout the whole night of 20 to 21 May, our infantry crossed over and formed in line between Aspern and Esling. At dawn on the 21st the Emperor toured the new dispositions and made some adjustments. He rested the left wing on Aspern, and filled the gap between this village and Esling with two lines of infantry (Lasalle's cavalry, meanwhile, had advanced 1,000 paces to the front). He ordered loopholes to be made in the wall of the cemetary, which stood right on the edge of Esling. Finally beyond Esling the right wing bent back almost at right angles from the main battle line, toward the Danube, facing the village of Enzerdorf. He did not occupy Enzerdorf, undoubtedly so as not to over-extend the line. On the right wing he placed the Grenadiers and Fusiliers of the Guard, and in reserve the Chasseurs à Cheval of the Guard and two squadrons of Polish Guard Horse. The Dragoons, Horse Grenadiers, and Gendarmes of the Guard were still on the far bank of the Danube with the Guard artillery. Only sixty pieces of artillery belonging to Marshal Massena's corps had crossed onto the Austrian bank. They were deployed in batteries between Aspern and Esling. We had no more than those sixty guns throughout the whole three days of the battle.

The Emperor made these defensive preparations while waiting for the arrival of the rest of the army. We had only about 30,000 men on the enemy bank, and were still waiting for Davout's corps, three divisions of cuirassiers, half of the Guard, most of the artillery, and the whole artillery park; in all, about 60,000 men.

---

7 An interesting digression which needs to be treated with caution. Lasalle lost the ground in this engagement, and we should be sceptical of claims that Austrian dead outnumbered French two to one. That said, Lasalle was not broken, and we must assume that the Austrians retired too if Chlapowski was able to walk over the ground that had been fought over. Nightfall was probably the reason why combat ended. The criticism of the Austrian hussars contrasts with the widely held view that the Austrian cavalry was among the best in Europe. But then Chlapowski admits that the Hungarian were much better mounted than the French. What matters to him is the control exercised by the French, which allowed them to retain order for longer. In this engagement, it is plausible that the more experienced French cavalry had the edge over a better mounted, but less experienced enemy. But this edge was not decisive. Chlapowski's generalization about Austrian performance in the whole campaign is harder to swallow, although the fact remains that regiment for regiment, the French had more recent experience of battle than their Austrian opponents. Chlapowski's perceptions were not clouded by chauvinism; pro-French he was, but he knew many Poles served in the Austrian cavalry!

FRENCH SWORDSMANSHIP AT ASPERN

At about mid-day the Austrians opened the battle along the whole front with a bombardment by several hundred cannon. Our cavalry, which had been standing in front of the infantry, was obliged to retreat and reformed in narrow columns a few hundred paces behind them. Our artillery replied, but at a ratio of one gun against three or four.

We saw lines of Austrian infantry all around us, but that day they did not attack our center. Instead they directed their main attack on Aspern, where, in addition to artillery fire, there were frequent and lively bouts of musketry.

From where we stood with the Emperor we were unable to see this attack, for a little wood blocked the view. I was sent several times with messages for Marshal Massena, who was defending Aspern, and I was able to study the Austrian columns. These were so deep that their superior numbers were very evident. The Austrians several times reached the edge of the village, but were always repulsed by point blank fire from the houses and gardens.

On one occasion I found Massena sitting down behind the wall of a house, resting. I gave him the Emperor's order and straight away he called for his horse and jumped into the saddle. But he found the right stirrup strap to be too short, and called his orderly to come and lengthen it. While waiting, Massena sat side-saddle, with his right leg resting on the horse's neck. At that moment a cannon ball struck the orderly stone dead and tore off the stirrup. The horse shied sideways and the Marshal tumbled into my arms. But he wasn't even bruised! Another strap was fixed, he remounted the horse and rode on.

Howitzer shells had set light to a dozen or so houses and nearly all the roofs were burning, but most of the houses and outbuildings were made of brick and so still provided good shelter for the infantry. Every time the Austrian columns got so close that it seemed the French bullets would no longer stop them, the French reserves charged with the bayonet. Not once did the Austrians withstand them, but fell immediately into disorder despite the fact that they were in column, and the French in line. The Austrians were happy to attack in column, as they had long since noticed that we had too little artillery; our infantry, on the other hand, advanced

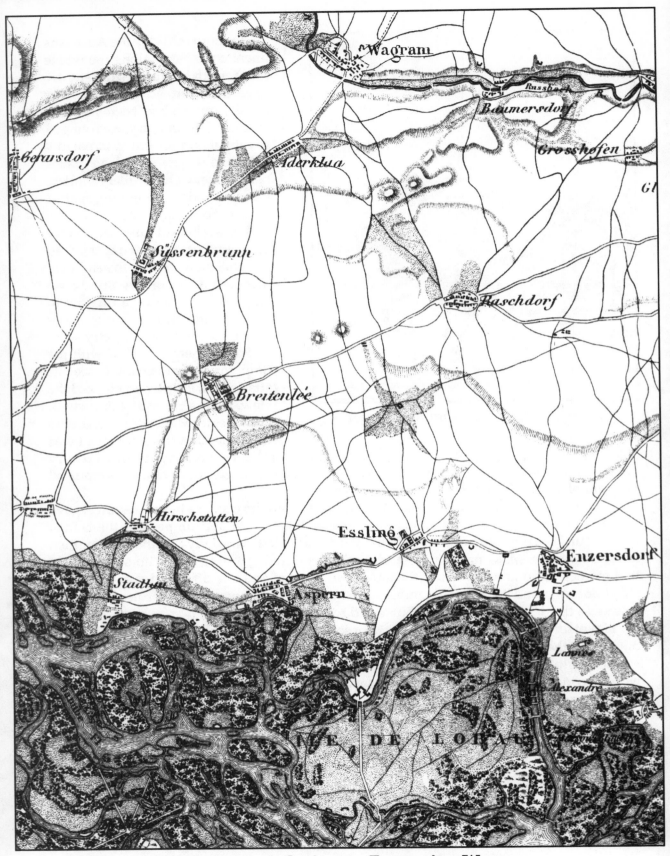

THE BATTLEFIELDS OF ASPERN, ESLING, AND WAGRAM

in line, almost at a run, because the enemy had many cannon behind its columns which fired canister in close support. That first day, the Austrians did not once enter the village.

The defense of Aspern convinced me of the superiority of French infantry over all others.

At about 5 P.M., the Emperor heard that the bridge spanning the second stretch of the Danube had been broken, just as a division of cuirassiers was passing across it. It had been smashed by boats laden with stones, launched by the Austrians from Stadelau, and carried along by the fast flowing current, which had been swollen by the melting snow from the mountains. But the bridge was repaired overnight and the rest of the cuirassier division passed across, followed by two of Oudinot's infantry divisions and the other half of the Guard. The next morning, therefore, we had about 60,000 men, but still no more than sixty guns. At dawn the Emperor mounted his horse and toured the lines. He gave command of the entire center to Marshal Lannes, and had all the infantry form column, except Massena's Corps in Aspern and the Guard, which he kept in reserve. He placed the sixty artillery pieces in the spaces between the columns, and behind them two divisions each of light cavalry and cuirassiers. When the attack was due to begin, the Emperor rode along the front of the army, raising his hat before each column and brandishing it in the enemy's direction. At this gesture, the columns replied with cheers, waving their shakos on the ends of their bayonets. Then the advance began all along the line.

About 1,000 paces away stood a screen of Austrian cavalry, with infantry behind. As our columns approached all these troops vanished, unmasking a grand battery which began firing. Soon their whole army appeared. It was advancing to meet us in columns, which on this occasion deployed into line a few hundred yards from us and began firing on the French columns. The enemy fired by battalion, one after another, just as a battalion would fire by companies. Their cannon were all firing canister. But nothing could stop the French columns.

FRENCH CUIRASSIERS ATTACKING AUSTRIAN INFANTRY AT ASPERN

They charged with the bayonet at the Austrian lines, which fell into disorder even before the French reached them.

The enemy artillery retired before our advance, stopping from time to time to fire canister. A great many Frenchmen fell, but they kept advancing, and the Austrians retreated before them. At last the enemy infantry took refuge behind a long line of Austrian cavalry, which our cavalry defeated two or three times, but which kept producing fresh regiments behind the broken ones. The enemy were still supported by their numerous artillery, which received every French attack with canister. Yet their line continued slowly to withdraw. From time to time the Austrian horse unmasked its infantry, which had either reformed or came up from reserve. Our cuirassiers twice reached this infantry and destroyed one or two battalions, but each time fresh regiments of Austrian horse arrived ready to attack, and our cuirassiers had to retire a few hundred paces to reform. The light cavalry divisions of Lasalle and Bruyere also charged a few times against far superior numbers of enemy cavalry. By eleven o'clock our infantry columns and cavalry had advanced nearly a mile. The cavalry would at one minute be advancing behind the infantry, and the next fighting out in front of it. Our formation reached the village of Breitenlee, where the rest of the Austrian army seemed to have gathered, for we could see more troops deploying to extend their right wing. Our line, advancing across open ground, was now shorter than the enemy's. As more and more Austrians were arriving, we became vulnerable to an outflanking attack. When I reported to the Emperor from Marshal Lannes that there were masses of enemy on our left wing which could outflank him, the Emperor placed two battalions of Old Guard in echelon in front of the village of Aspern, but still a long way behind Lannes' left flank, which they were supposed to be securing. Meanwhile, more of our army were crossing the repaired bridge. The Emperor was counting on the arrival of Davout's corps, with another sixty cannon, the third cuirassier division, another light cavalry division, the rest of the Guard and finally the reserve artillery park. Together with Lannes' corps, Davout's corps would have brought our numbers level with the enemy. But at around midday, the news arrived, first that both bridges were again down, and soon after that Marshal Lannes had been badly wounded, and had lost one leg while the other had been pulverized. Soon after Oudinot also went down with several wounds, none of them mortal, but he was forced to quit the field.

With blood-chilling coolness the Emperor gave the order to retire to our starting position between Aspern and Esling. This withdrawal was carried out in good order. A few times the Austrian cavalry attacked at certain points along our retreating line. They were always repulsed with losses by Lasalles' light cavalry, which was supported by cuirassiers in the second line. The enemy could not break through anywhere, and our infantry did not even have to halt to receive cavalry. Not once did our cuirassiers seek shelter behind the infantry. At about 3 P.M. our army was back in its original position between Aspern and Esling. By that time our artillery was having to cut down drastically on ammunition expenditure. The two cuirassier divisions retired behind our infantry to escape the attention of the enemy guns, and formed up in two lines before the Emperor. But the enemy cannon still hit them, and soon their shots were even reaching the banks of the Danube to our rear, and several struck the wounded who were waiting there. So the wounded were gathered at the bridgehead, and it would take two days to ferry them all back to Lobau.

Once our infantry had regained its positions between Aspern and Esling, the Emperor ordered the two battalions of Old Guard Grenadiers to transfer to the right flank opposite

FRENCH INFANTRY AT ESLING

Enzerdorf, for he had seen enemy columns advancing in that direction and these troops, apparently Liechtenstein's corps, had in fact occupied Enzersdorf and were right on the banks of the Danube.

So now the Austrian army was in a semi-circle around us. Marshal Bellegarde had his right flank on the Danube and his left before Aspern; Archduke Charles was in the center with the main army; and Liechtenstein made up their left flank opposite and nearly behind our right wing, which consisted only of four battalions of Chasseurs, and two of Grenadiers of the Old Guard, with two squadrons each of Polish lancers and the Chasseurs à Cheval of the Guard to their rear. These half dozen battalions and four squadrons so overawed Liechtenstein that he did not press home his attack, and so they protected our lines of retreat.[8] The Poles performed very well, despite heavy losses. In this position shots from Bellegarde's cannon, flying over Aspern, were hitting our right wing, and Liechtenstein's cannon, which were also firing too high, were hitting our left wing. The Emperor, standing with his staff behind the center, was being fired on from all three sides, but most of the shots flew over our heads. But some heavy canister did reach the cuirassiers standing 500 paces in front of the Emperor.

8 Liechtenstein's caution is understandable. The French Guard, especially its Old Guard infantry, engendered a healthy respect from the armies of Napoleon's adversaries.

AUSTRIAN ASSAULT ON ASPERN

We could no longer return the enemy's artillery fire by this time, for of the sixty pieces that had been brought across the bridge many had been dismounted, and all had used up their ammunition. But not one piece was taken by the enemy.

The Emperor stood rooted to the spot, the reins of his horse forgotten and telescope in hand, issuing orders and despatching us in all directions. Very few of us had fresh horses left, and my last one was very tired, so when I was sent to Marshal Massena, who was nearby, I preferred to go on foot, leading my horse by the reins. The Emperor had observed that a strong column from Archduke Charles' command, that is, the center, was advancing on Aspern. I was to warn Marshal Massena of this and advise him to create a reserve column to deal with it.

The Marshal was sitting under a tree by the wall of a burnt out house (only a very few houses were standing by then). He mounted his horse immediately and formed a column in the open ground just as the Austrians reached the village. They far outnumbered the defenders. The French infantry in the houses poured point blank fire into them, but this time both Austrian columns with their yellow standards waving at their heads kept coming forward and occupied the buildings and gardens on the edge of the village. Massena drew his sword and led the column he had just organized in a counter-attack. The Frenchmen who had been ejected from the houses attached themselves to the column's flanks.

Without firing a shot, this column fell upon the Austrians, who had been disorganized by entering the village, and it wrought dreadful execution with the bayonet.

When I returned to the Emperor, there were so many bodies lying in the village street that my horse was obliged to tread on them. Of course, in addition to the Austrians, a great many Frenchmen had fallen there during the day from musketry and cannon fire.

I was able to deliver to the Emperor Massena's report that Aspern had been saved, and that the Marshal expected to hold out until nightfall. Next I was sent to Esling and after that to the positions facing Enzersdorf, so only later did I learn that the Austrian infantry had got into Aspern three more times that afternoon, and each time had been ejected by a courageous effort.

But at the same time the Austrian center had formed columns to assault Esling. General Durosnel, the Emperor's a.d.c. who commanded our troops there, rode forward to reconnoiter the enemy. But as his horse was exhausted, he was unable to escape an attack by Austrian cuirassiers, and was taken prisoner. An intense artillery barrage alerted us to the attack on Esling. A column of Austrian grenadiers, flags unfurled, with their officers on horseback riding at their front, advanced on the village.

The fire from the cemetary and houses did not stop them. They fell upon the French, who were forced to retreat. The Emperor ordered General Mouton, another of his a.d.c.s, to take four battalions of Guard Chasseurs from the right wing and retake Esling. They did so without firing a shot. Once again, the cemetary was littered with Hungarian bodies as Aspern had been. Esling stayed in our hands until evening.

Just as night fell, the Austrians launched one more attack in four infantry columns against our center between Aspern and Esling. Our infantry were tired and thirsty, and had been sheltering in the ditches that ran besides the road from Esling to Aspern. When the Austrian columns approached, our men were roused by the drums and returned to the ranks, fixed bayonets, and advanced at the double to counterattack the enemy. They came forward with such determination that the enemy columns fell into confusion and began to retire. Our cuirassiers, advancing at the trot because our horses could barely manage to move, passed between our battalions and would have charged, but the Austrian horse deployed immediately in front of its foot, advanced to within 500 paces and halted. It was beginning to grow dark. The Emperor ordered the cuirassiers and light infantry to retire across the bridge to the island of Lobau. The wounded were crossing in a constant stream. After the cavalry, those cannons and limbers which still had wheels crossed over, some drawn by only one pair of horses. I counted forty pieces, and concluded the other twenty must have been left behind for lack of teams. The Emperor stood by the bridge. At about 10 P.M. he crossed over to the island with the Guard. There, they brought Marshal Lannes before him. He embraced Lannes repeatedly, and in the clear night I could see that he was crying.[9]

At midnight Massena's infantry and Oudinot's grenadiers and voltigeurs also crossed the bridge, which was immediately dismantled. 60,000 men had taken part in the battle, and there were now only 30,000 soldiers on the island present and under arms. We had lost half our numbers in dead and wounded. This was the bloodiest battle in the annals of French military history, and undoubtedly the most glorious testament to French valor even though they lost the day and had to retreat leaving the enemy in possession of the field.

At about 2 A.M. the Emperor crossed by raft from Lobau to the south bank of the Danube.

---

9 Lannes seemed to rally over the following days, but gangrene developed. He died on May 31. He was perhaps the best of Napoleon's marshals.

NAPOLEON CROSSING FROM LOBAU TO THE SOUTH BANK OF THE DANUBE

We crossed over behind him on two more rafts, but the currents were strong and fast and carried us half a mile downstream, so we only reached Ebersdorf on foot at about 5 a.m.

We found Marshal Davout's corps at Ebersdorf. The Emperor ordered him to stand to arms immediately and march toward Presburg to occupy the outskirts of the town and prevent Archduke Charles from crossing the Danube there. For Charles could have crossed the bridge in force, defeated Davout, and taken all the troops on Lobau island prisoner, along with the wounded.

Early the next day the Emperor sent me after Marshal Davout. His march to Presburg took him three days, and on the third he attacked and took the village of Engeran on the edge of the town. I returned immediately with this news to Ebersdorf. On receiving it, the Emperor transferred his quarters to Schoenbrunn. Over the next few days the Guard was ferried back from Lobau island on rafts, and its infantry billeted at Schoenbrunn, while the cavalry encamped in surrounding villages. After we had returned to Schoenbrunn on the 27th, an a.d.c. arrived from Prince Eugene Beauharnais with the news that he was pursuing Archduke John, whom he had defeated a number of times in Italy and forced to retreat, and was now only fifteen miles from Vienna with his army of 40,000 men. The a.d.c. who brought this news, named Bataille, had been sent to Neustadt with an escort of cavalry to inform the Emperor of Eugene's approach and request orders.

The a.d.c. was sent right back to the Prince, who meanwhile was pursuing Archduke John through Oedinburg and Steinamanger, or Szombathely in Hungarian. The Archduke joined forces with an army newly formed in Hungary, and occupied a favorable position near Sabadeggi, three hours from Raab. Prince Eugene immediately attacked him there and after a day's battle, forced him to abandon the place. By evening the Army of Italy had reached the town of Raab, which was surrounded with old defenses. Archduke John left 3,000 men to hold our army up for a few days, while he retreated three miles and crossed the Danube at Komorn.

Before the Battle of Raab took place the Emperor had first sent me to Marshal Davout at Presburg, to inform him of Prince Eugene's march through Hungary toward Raab and to advise him to make contact with his right wing. Then I was to go with a cavalry escort to Prince Eugene and bring news from him straight back to the Emperor. I journeyed by post chaise to the Marshal, who gave me a horse for the next leg. I then went to his light cavalry, which was already on Hungarian soil on the road from Haimburg to Raab, and selected only fifteen of his best-mounted hussars to escort me. At Kitsee I turned right off the main road, understanding from the Emperor that Prince Eugene would still be in the region of Papa. I had copied out the route from Kitsee to Papa from the Emperor's master map. At nightfall I arrived at the first village and requested a guide, and I was delighted and astonished to hear the peasants speaking a slavic dialect. They too were very pleased to hear me speaking Polish. They immediately summoned someone who had been in Raab that day, but they told me that the French had already defeated the Austrians at Raab and were in possession of the town. I asked if one of them could take me to the French army at Raab. A few offered with great alacrity, and none asked if I would pay them. The Slavic nature is everywhere the same. They offered me and my hussars wine, bread, and ham. They were much cheered by the Austrian defeat. They said they had been told by their forefathers that their region had once been part of Poland and they wanted to be reunited, now they had heard that the French Emperor intended restoring Poland. This was an interesting demonstration that folk traditions die very hard. None, even among the older men present, knew in what age their region had been linked with Poland. Could this have been in the days of King Ludwig? Or even earlier? Whenever, there was no doubt that the local Slavs were well disposed toward the Poles and there was not a Magyar among them.[10]

I wrote to Marshal Davout reporting what the peasants had told me about Raab and asked him to send an officer with the news straight to Schoenbrunn. I assured him we could trust the information, as it came from Slavic peasants who were friendly toward us. I also sent back my hussar escort, who could confirm what I said, as I trusted the locals and would reach the Army of Italy sooner if I travelled alone by carriage.

I reached Raab at about 10 p.m., just as the Prince was entering the city, which had surrendered after a two day bombardment.

After a short rest in the town, Prince Eugene went to the palace outside the walls where his headquarters had been established and where the Italian Guard was waiting for him. The Guard consisted of two battalions of Grenadiers and two of Chasseurs, with the Lombard Guard of Honor, consisting of about a hundred horsemen. Over lunch the Prince, Marshal Macdonald (who was under his command) and the Chief of Staff, Gifflongen, gave me a detailed account of the Battle of Raab, which I noted down to tell the Emperor. I went into the town after lunch, but could find no carriage at the post house. I had already resolved to return on horseback, when a portly citizen in a sheepskin coat approached me, and offered to lend me his carriage to take me to Vienna.

---

10 There is no record that this region was ever ruled by Poland. This may be a folk memory of some Slavic king before the Hapsburgs.

"And how shall I return it to you?" I asked.

"Don't worry," he replied. "I am only happy to be of service." As he had spoken to me in quite good Polish, I asked if he was Hungarian. "No," he answered. "I am Slovenian. I could tell you were Polish and hence a fellow countryman. And on top of that you are with the Emperor with whose help we hope to free ourselves from foreign domination."

"Thank you very much, sir. But please tell me to whom in Vienna I should return the carriage."

"I don't know anybody in Vienna. Do what you wish with the carriage when you have no more use for it."

While we talked the horses were harnessed, I thanked this citizen sincerely and set off in my fine Hungarian carriage. During the night, about half way to Vienna, I reached Marshal Davout's outposts. The next afternoon I reached Schoenbrunn and submitted a full report to the Emperor.

Immediately after the Battle of Esling, the Emperor ordered a pontoon bridge to be built across the first stream of the Danube, and two more across the middle stream to the island of Lobau. The third stream was much narrower. The material for six bridges to cross the last stream was prepared on Lobau island.

Every day marching columns arrived from France,[11] made up of entire companies and battalions destined for every regiment in the army. These columns were made up partly of recovered sick and wounded who had been convalescing in towns from Ratisbon to Vienna, and partly of conscripts from France. Most of the men in these columns were sent out to the island of Lobau, to bring the badly depleted corps there back up to strength.

The three bridges were constructed throughout the month of June. All this time the Emperor stayed at Schoenbrunn, but he rode out nearly every day, most often to Ebersdorf, to oversee the construction of the bridges. He also toured the camps that had been set up around Vienna. During this time we were visited frequently by officers from our allied armies. We even received some Russians, a major Gorgoli, a very civil gentleman, and a Lieutenant Colonel Czerniczeff. One Swedish officer also came, but most of our visitors were Germans. We received several Polish officers sent by Prince Poniatowski,. But the man whose visits worried me most was not any Polish officer, but Mr. Ignacy Potocki. I don't know why the Emperor had summoned him. They had a few conversations without witnesses. He was an uncommonly reserved, polished, and reflective man, the exact opposite of his father, Stanislaw, whom I had known in Warsaw and Paris. Mr. Ignacy Potocki did not seem satisfied with his audiences with the Emperor and returned to Warsaw very dispirited.[12]

The Imperial Staff would often go into Vienna, but the Emperor would only pass through the city if his route took him there. Actors from the Vienna Opera performed a few evenings a week in the theater at Schoenbrunn. Besides officers, civilians from Vienna would also request tickets to attend. Overall I did find the behavior of these people strange. When I went to the theater in Vienna, I would find it full of society ladies, and outside would be many

11 "Marches de colonnes" in the original. These were ad hoc military formations, created for the duration of a march from the rear areas to the army. On arrival they would be broken up and their component units absorbed by combat formations. They provided protection, discipline and administration for replacements going to the front.

12 Potocki had come on behalf of a group of Polish deputies, who were seeking Napoleon's support for the elevation of the Duchy of Warsaw to the Kingdom of Poland and the restoration of Polish lands.

elegant carriages with ladies and gentlemen dressed in all their finery, as if the French occupation was a matter of supreme indifference to them. It had not been like that when the Austrians had occupied Warsaw.[13] Then, the distress had been shared at all levels of society. But we must remember that the Austrian nobility had left Vienna before the French had arrived, and that the populace which I saw in the theater and promenading in town consisted mainly of merchants, many of the Jews, and their wives. However, I did hear of some ladies of noble family who had remained behind and had a fine time with the French. Vienna and its surroundings appeared as if all was at perfect peace. The French employed lots of artisans, especially carriage builders, and so these were very content. I myself bought a light carriage.

During this time I was again sent to Raab. I had orders for both Marshal Davout and Prince Eugene, which the Emperor had quickly dictated to me. Traveling from Davout to Raab, I found our light cavalry billeted along the whole length of the road, and everywhere they were getting on famously with the locals. Here I saw some Frenchmen dancing under the trees with some Slovakian girls, and these local urchins were playing in French uniforms, which the soldiers were quite happy for them to dress up in. All along my route there was bustle and cheer, and when I spoke to the Slovakian coach drivers in Polish, they were happy to drive at a cracking pace.

On 1 July the bridges were finished. They were good and solid. On 2 July the Emperor crossed to the island of Lobau and moved back under canvas. Prince Eugene arrived with his corps on the 3 July. He had sent three battalions in extended columns marching from Raab to Komorn, so that the Austrians would see them. Marshal Davout had performed the same ruse, sending a few battalions eastwards along the bank of the Danube, but all these troops took roundabout routes which eventually brought them back to rejoin their corps.

The island of Lobau was a fine sight. It is covered with trees, with open ground between them. Everywhere the French soldiers had built pretty little huts. There were no proper houses on the island, which in normal times was uninhabited.

On 3 July such a heavy rain fell that the Emperor did not leave his tent. This consisted of three tents joined together. The first was our duty room where we also slept. The middle room contained the Emperor's bed, a small table, a few chairs and some poles from which hung his maps. The rear tent was occupied by his secretary, and normally by some of his household.

It rained all night. When, in the early hours of morning, the Emperor emerged from the tent, he turned to the grenadier standing to the right of the entrance (there were always two on guard who would present arms when the Emperor appeared), and said:

"My friend, what dreadful weather." To which the grenadier replied:

"It's better than no weather at all."

In the afternoon of 4 July the weather brightened. That evening, 6,000 grenadiers and voltigeurs embarked in specially prepared boats, and skirting around the right of the island crossed the last channel of the Danube. They wore white armbands to help recognition in the dark. They landed to the east of Enzersdorf, and were unopposed by the enemy who had been prepared for us to cross at the same point as we had done before the Battle of Aspern. The Emperor had seen them install a battery within cannon shot of that crossing, and this was why he decided to cross three quarters of a mile further to the right. Once the 6,000 grenadiers and

13 In the opening rounds of the 1809 campaign in Galicia, Prince Poniatowski abandoned Warsaw, and the city was briefly occupied by the Austrians. They were obliged to withdraw when Poniatowski drove south against their lines of communications.

voltigeurs had landed, at about 10 p.m., the six pre-prepared bridges were immediately thrown across, and by 2 A.M. our army had already started to cross. Two bridges were used only by infantry, two by cavalry, and two by the artillery. The columns were so organized that the crossing was made in the greatest order and by 6 A.M. six corps had reached the far bank. On the right stood Marshal Davout, then Oudinot, then Bernadotte's Saxons, then the Army of Italy (three weak corps) in the center, and Marshal Massena on the left. The Guard, the Bavarian corps, and Marmont's 10,000 men from Illyria made up the very large reserve. These corps crossed the bridges last of all and I didn't see them before 5 p.m. That same day Baraguay d'Hilliers, who had remained facing Presburg, together with Eugene's three battalions from Raab, appeared within the enemy's sight marching eastward. This fooled Archduke John, who had arrived at Presburg, to march back toward Komorn, thus distancing himself further from Archduke Charles' main army, and so his army of 50,000 men would not arrive in time for the battle of Wagram on 6 July.

The Emperor believed that the Austrians would still be in position in the fortifications they had built between Aspern and Esling. He therefore formed his army, once all the troops were across, in two lines with their left wing on Enzersdorf, ready to take Archduke Charles in the flank. But when the Archduke got news that we had crossed at a different point than he had expected, he vacated his defences and chose a position in the hills behind Wagram, with his right flank on the Danube.

At 8 A.M. on 5 July all our troops began to advance. All we could see was enemy cavalry retiring slowly before us. We advanced like this all day, never knowing where we would find the Austrian army. Then, at 5 P.M., we finally saw their infantry on the high ground to right and left of Wagram. Bernadotte's Saxons advanced straight on the town itself, and entered it just as darkness fell. Meanwhile, Oudinot's grenadiers and voltigeurs, having come up on the Saxon's right and approached Wagram from that side, mistook their white uniforms for Austrians and began firing into the town. Before the French commanders realized their mistake, they had killed a great many Saxons, who, recognizing the French uniforms, had not returned their fire. Those Saxons who survived were so unnerved by this attack that they panicked and fled. The entire Saxon corps was so disorganized that it could not be rallied that night.

As night fell, Marshal Davout's right wing stumbled upon the Austrian left and immediately attacked. Realizing that the whole of Archduke Charles' army was before him, the Emperor sent officers to all corps with orders to halt where they were and cook their evening meal.

A number of drums were stacked three high together, and the Emperor's tent was stretched across them. He lay down beneath it, while the rest of his staff slept in the open.

We were woken at 4 A.M. on 6 July by the Emperor's servants, bringing an invitation to dine. A few paces from the Imperial tent we found food in abundance laid out on saddle cloths on the ground. It was a feast worthy of Paris, with soup, several different dishes and every kind of wine. As the night before we had eaten only what we happened to have with us or had been able to scrounge from the Emperor's kitchen, we devoured this picnic with gusto, joking amongst ourselves that this would surely be the last time that all of us would be together at such a feast.

We were still enjoying this breakfast, reclining on the ground like ancient Romans, when the Austrians began their attack on Davout, thus attacking our right wing with their left. This began with a heavy artillery bombardment. At the same moment our whole army stood to

BATTLE OF WAGRAM

arms, and regimental bands began playing reveille all along the line. Soon they were drowned out by the roar of the cannon. It grew lighter and we mounted our horses, but we did not move from our position. The most beautiful sight I have ever seen in my life then unfurled before our eyes. Within a radius of about a mile, we could see the entire Austrian army, with its right flank anchored on the Danube, and its left extending beyond Wagram, as well as our own army with its left flank at Aspen and the rest of the line running parallel with the enemy. Our army was in the same deployment as it had been the night before. To recap, Massena commanded the left wing. To his right was the Army of Italy, and beyond them the Saxons, now only in brigade strength, as the rest had been sent to the rear. Then came Oudinot to the right of Wagram, Davout formed the right wing and further to his right was a division of light cavalry with a cuirassier division to the rear. The entire Guard was in reserve in the center, behind the Army of Italy, and to its right, behind Oudinot, were two division of cuirassiers. Behind the Guard were two divisions of Bavarians (their third division was in the Tyrol), Marmont's corps and the remainder of the Saxons, who had been restored to order after the

Napoleon And Staff At Wagram

previous night. The Emperor was undoubtedly keeping these corps in reserve in case Archduke John should approach.

The Austrian attack on Davout on our right wing turned out to be a feint, and their real attack, with far greater numbers, was directed at Massena on the left.

By 6 a.m., along the whole length of the mile-long battle front, the artillery of both sides was firing louder than I had ever heard before. You could see the fire and smoke all the way from the left wing by the river, past Oudinot to the right of Wagram, and as far as Davout on the right. The ground was completely flat from the Danube as far as Oudinot, then where Davout stood it became hilly. The Emperor stood unmoving on his grey horse behind the Army of Italy, telescope in hand. Berthier alone stood beside him, and right behind them two of us orderly officers. Behind us, in turn stood two Chasseurs of the Guard, one with the map case, and the other with a great big telescope. As soon as the Emperor sent one of us off with an order, another would come up and take his place. For all the orderly officers, together with Berthier's a.d.c.s, stood 150 paces behind the Emperor, so our large numbers would not attract the enemy's fire.

The two lines advanced closer to each other. By about 8 A.M. Davout's right wing had made good progress, and the Austrian left under Rosenberg was already in retreat. But the Austrian right, by the Danube, was meanwhile continuing to advance. This was Archduke Charles' main attack. After a thunderous bombardment he had launched deep assault columns at Massena, who had been obliged by the force of the attack to retire toward Enzersdorf. The Austrians followed up at a cracking pace, and a large body of Austrian horse appeared on their left to protect their open flank. At the head of this body eight regiments of hussars, dragoons and cuirassiers charged Lasalles' light cavalry division and broke it. General Lasalle himself died in the charge. It was clear that the enemy had directed the greater part of his forces against our left, with no lesser intention than to cut us off from our bridges and in one blow destroy or capture our whole army. But in making this massive attack with his right wing he extended his line too far and weakened his center.

When the Emperor saw that Massena's corps was retreating and already beginning to fall into disorder, he rode off at a gallop to join him. We found Marshal Massena with the last of his retreating columns. He was sitting in a light open carriage, as he was weak from old wounds, but he was still in the thick of the fighting. The Emperor gave him the following order: "If the Austrians don't stop, retreat as far as the bridges. If they continue their advance, I'll have them surrendering within the hour." He then turned around and galloped back to his vantage point. He rode along the front of Lasalles' cavalry, in between the main line and the skirmishers.

Between Lasalles' cavalry and the Italian corps stood a brigade of Saxon cavalry, which was retiring after losing heavily to enemy cannon fire. The Emperor ordered them to halt and face the enemy, and taking out his watch he said to their commander: "All I ask is that you withstand this fire for another thirty minutes. By then, the firing will be over."

Then he gave the following orders: the Polish Lancers supported by the Chasseurs à Cheval of the Guard were to advance at the gallop in front of the left wing of the Army of Italy; the Horse Artillery of the Guard were to follow them, deploy on their left and fire into the flank of the Austrians attacking Massena; Macdonald[14] was to form attack columns and advance on the left of Wagram followed by two cuirassier divisions, and Davout was ordered to send over the third cuirassier division to bring up the rear. Napoleon placed all this cavalry under the command of Marshal Bessieres, but as he did so the Marshal's horse was hit in the shoulder by an enemy cannon ball. We thought the Marshal too had been killed, but he was only concussed. When he fell with his horse, the Emperor simply turned away, called General Nansouty to him and repeated the same orders he had given to Bessieres: as soon as Macdonald broke the enemy center, he was to exploit the victory with two of his divisions, and with the third division sent over by Davout, he was to attack the Austrians pursuing Massena on the left. He added that they would soon begin their retreat and that he would support Nansouty with the cavalry of the Guard.

Once the Guard Horse Artillery had deployed its sixty guns and fired a few salvoes at the enemy, their own artillery fire slackened considerably. This was well within the half hour promised by the Emperor. It was also clear that there was no stopping Macdonald, who was making good progress with the cuirassiers advancing behind.

The Emperor called me to him and told me to deliver orders, first, to the Polish Guard Horse to charge the enemy facing them, and second, to the Guard Chasseurs to support the charge. When he had finished speaking and I raised my hat in salute, as was our custom on

14 Macdonald, the reader will recall, was with the Army of Italy.

THE POLES AT WAGRAM

receiving orders from the Emperor, a cannon ball hit my shako and hurled it through the air. The Emperor roared with laughter and said to me: "It's a good job you're not taller!" Then he gave me a further order, to go straight from the cavalry to Macdonald and tell him that the Austrian right had not only been halted, but was beginning to retreat, and order him to brush aside everything in front of him. "Stay with Macdonald," he said in conclusion, "and come back at a triple gallop," (a phrase of his he used to mean very quickly) "to tell me what happens." A colleague of mine dismounted, dusted off my shako and handed it to me. It hadn't been marked in any way, so the ball must have been spent. I recount this little incident to show that the Emperor was cool headed enough to make jokes even at a tense moment like that.

I reached the Chasseurs and Polish Horse, and delivered the order to General Kaminski. Straight away he launched a charge against the Schwarzenburg Ulans and Latour Dragoons. I did not take part in the charge, because I had to go on immediately to Macdonald, but I later learnt that it succeeded. During this charge an incident occurred that would have brought disaster to the regiment, had it not been for the presence of mind of Lieutenant Colonel Kozietulski. The front two squadrons were commanded by Colonel Delaitre, a Frenchman, and the other two by Kozietulski. Delaitre was short-sighted and wore spectacles. Seeing the Austrian lancers preparing to charge, and overestimating their strength, he decided that the regiment should retire on the Chasseurs who were in support to the rear. As senior officer present, he ordered the entire regiment to turn right about face. Kozietulski saw the danger that the Austrians would catch the regiment from behind, and so he immediately gave exactly the same order again. He had a fine loud voice, and was well respected in the regiment, and luckily was obeyed. So having twice turned about face, our lancers again found themselves facing the enemy. Immediately they completed this pirouette, Kozietulski ordered: "Prepare you weapons! Advance at the trot!" The ensuing charge succeeded, and Delaitre later thanked Kozietulski most sincerely.

The regiment captured 150 ulans and a few officers, including their colonel, the Duke of Auersberg, but our officers admitted that they had been easy to catch, as the ulans had let themselves be captured when they recognized their fellow countrymen. Normally one regiment could never capture 150 horsemen in one charge on an open battlefield. To catch such a bag the pursuit would generally have to be longer, or the enemy trapped by some obstacle.

KOZIETULSKI

The positions of the two armies had now changed considerably. Our left wing was far to the rear, our center three-quarters of a mile forward with the gap between center and rear filled by the artillery and cavalry of the Guard, and our right wing also far advanced.

Archduke Charles, seeing no doubt that although the attack by his right wing against Massena had succeeded, it was now in danger of being cut off by our center, must have ordered it to retreat. It is important to remember that whoever hopes to outflank his enemy in turn makes himself vulnerable to outflanking, because by his maneuver he exposes his own flank. It's true that the Archduke had a strong reserve behind his center which gave Macdonald a tough time, but either he wanted to conserve it, or he had been unnerved by Macdonald's steady advance. Whatever the reason, Macdonald told me when I reached him that the Austrians had not once stood to receive his bayonet charges. I myself could see that they were retreating all along the line, despite the fact that they should have made a stand in the center until their right wing, which wasn't even in sight, had retired to join them. As it was, Macdonald kept moving forward and the enemy tried in vain to hold him with cannon fire.

I stayed with Macdonald for over an hour, waiting for some important news to take back, but knowing the Emperor was anxious for a report from that direction, I could wait no longer and returned. I reported that I had seen Austrian columns retreating by the Danube, which the Emperor was unable to see from his position because our artillery and the French and Austrian cavalry blocked his line of sight to the left wing. However, above the din he could intermittently hear the sound of small arms fire moving from the direction of Enzersdorf toward Stadelau, which suggested that the Austrians were retreating. Shortly after I arrived, one of my colleagues returned from Massena with the news that the Austrians were in full retreat and that Massena was pursuing them. It was by then about 6 P.M. I don't think the Emperor had expected Archduke John to be fooled by the trick of marching a few battalions in the direction of Komorn, and he expected any minute that John would arrive to the aid of Archduke Charles. Because of this the Emperor still kept 40,000 men, that is, the Guard, Marmont, and the Bavarians, in reserve.

From 6 P.M. the fighting moved steadily away from us and cannonballs were no longer reaching our position, even though the firing was as dense as it had been an hour before.

At about 7 P.M. the Emperor sent me off to Macdonald again with orders to return only when the Marshal had made camp for the night. There was no urgent message to deliver, and all my horses were tired, so I set off at a trot. All around me were dead bodies, and here and there I found wounded men who had not yet been treated by the medical services. I saw many who were unable to lift themselves, who called to me for help. Our surgeons were doing what they could, but were unable to help them all. When I had changed horses, the Imperial page had given me wine for my flask, which I kept in one of my saddle holsters because I thought it enough in Germany to have only one pistol.[15] I dismounted from time to time to give drinks to the thirsty, and shared out some bread and ham which I kept in my saddle bag.

On my way to Macdonald I rode past all three cuirassier divisions, which were marching quietly after the infantry.

As soon as I reached him, Macdonald told me he was very unhappy with the cavalry and instructed me to tell the Emperor from him that if the cuirassiers had done their duty, we would have taken 30,000 prisoners.

---

15 Whereas in Spain's guerilla war, a lone officer like Chlapowski would be wise to be heavily armed.

As it was getting dark, the infantry halted for the night by the village of Stammersdorf. I returned to the Emperor at about 10 P.M. I found him dining with General Berthier in his proper tent, not the hurried shelter of the night before. I gave my report and had to repeat the message from Macdonald about the cavalry. The Emperor made no comment about that.

I found my colleagues also at supper, and they had saved some food for me. Comparing notes about the day, we found that one of our number, Alfred de Noailles, had died, and another was wounded. Fully half of our horses had been lost.

The next day we also lost another colleague, the Prince Salm-Kyrbourg. His aunt was the Princess Hohenzollern Sigmaringen, who had cared for Prince Eugene Beauharnais and his sister, Queen Hortense, when their mother had left them. The Princess had lived in Paris for some years, and enjoyed great favor for looking after the Emperor's step-children. It appears she had asked the Emperor to take the young Salm-Kyrbourg as an orderly officer. This young man, no more than twenty years old, was very self-important, wore a great star on his chest representing some Bavarian Order, and took great offence at the slightest insult. As a Prince of the Rhine Confederation he had decided that all soldiers on guard duty should present arms when he passed, and he gave instructions to this effect to their commanding officers. These of course had simply laughed in his face. During the Battle of Wagram the Emperor had given him an order to despatch, and according to his custom with new orderly officers, had told him to repeat back the order to show he had understood it properly. Apparently Salm had either babbled some incoherence back, or given one of the marshals a garbled order. Anyway, the upshot was that he left the next day. Perhaps the Emperor sent him away, or he decided the work was not to his liking. Whatever the reason, we never saw him again. In his place the Emperor appointed Watteville, a very experienced officer. This had been the only occasion on which the Emperor had appointed an orderly officer who had never served in one of the main arms of service. Most of us came from the artillery and engineers. The a.d.c.s also had to have served at least two years with a regiment, to gain experience and be able to deliver orders and report intelligently what they saw.

At midnight we were woken by a great uproar from behind Marshal Davout's corps on the right. The Emperor and all his staff mounted up and he sent some of us off in the direction of the shouting. We came back over the next half to three quarters of an hour with reports that many of our soldiers were running about without their weapons, shouting that Archduke John was upon us. But the Emperor was not disturbed by these stories, as that morning he had sent a light cavalry division to March [Morawa], a town this side of Presburg, to watch for Archduke John's arrival. As they had reported nothing, and the Guard was positioned to protect our rear, the Emperor went back to bed. It turned out that this nonsense had been started by French soldiers foraging for food and hay in the night, who had run across some Bavarian soldiers doing the same thing, and on hearing them speaking German had fled in panic spreading the rumor which had eventually reached us. They had quietened down within the hour. This episode shows that when near to the enemy you should never let soldiers go foraging on their own.[16] If it is essential to find food because the soldiers have none, special detachments should be formed under experienced officers. The Emperor's army was always

16 It also shows that even the soldiers of a victorious army were prone to panic when rumors flew at nighttime. This incident, together with Oudinot's assault on his Saxon allies the evening before, demonstrates the dangers inherent in a polyglot army. In 1809, the French were still not used to serving with allied troops in the main army, as on previous campaigns, with some notable exceptions, Napoleon had tended to use allies for rear area or detached operations.

MARSHAL MACDONALD

disorganized in this respect. Only Davout's corps distinguished itself by its self-restraint and order.

After the battle the army certainly needed a rest, but I was surprised that the Emperor did not order the pursuit to begin at 7 A.M. the next day, as he usually would. He only mounted his horse at about 8 A.M., and ordered only two of us, Fodoas and I, to ride behind him with his inseparable mameluke, Roustam, and two chasseurs. He rode slowly over the battlefield. There were lots of dead soldiers, and we still found a few alive but badly wounded. The Emperor stopped several times by these men, and ordered Roustam to give them some wine or brandy and a bit of bread from the supplies Roustam used to carry for the Emperor. Ambulances were picking up the wounded and the surgeons were working among them. Soon Roustam told the Emperor his supplies had run out, and the Emperor set off at a gallop to Macdonald's position half a mile away. Macdonald had seen us coming from some way off and rode out to meet us. The Emperor clasped his hand, placed it over his own heart and said, "Macdonald, you have returned to my heart. I appoint you Marshal of France." I should explain that the two men had been estranged for a few years, apparently from the time of the trial of General Moreau. They rode together along the front of one of Macdonald's infantry regiments, I believe it was the 10th Regiment of the Line. Macdonald told the Emperor that, the day before, this regiment had conducted such brilliant bayonet charges against the Austrian reserve that for an hour and a half it had overthrown every regiment which barred its way. The Emperor thereupon ordered that this regiment should have the inscription on its guidons [little flags used for drill]: "One against ten" [un contre dix].

From Macdonald, the Emperor rode out to our forward pickets at Stammersdorf. This is the first staging post on the road from Vienna to Brunn and Prague. It stands on a hill, with a good view all round. The Emperor dismounted there and scanned the horizon with his telescope. After a few minutes he caught sight of a small cavalry detachment coming toward us from the direction of the enemy with a column of soldiers on foot. At length, they arrived at our position. They turned out to be an officer and his platoon of chasseurs à cheval returning from pre-dawn patrol, with a dozen or so Polish deserters from the Austrian army who, according to the officer, had emerged from the bushes unarmed, waving a white cloth. The Emperor told me to find out their regiment and corps, where they had fought the day before, and where their regiment was heading? They could answer the first questions but did not know where their corps was marching because they had hidden in the first wood they passed through during the night. They added that there must be a great many more Poles in hiding, as they had often discussed with Galicians in other regiments the intention to desert to the French. The Emperor told me to ask if they wanted to serve with him. They replied: "That's why we changed sides. We knew there were Polish regiments serving with you." In actual fact, there weren't any, apart from the Guard Lancers. The Emperor asked me which was the most senior Polish officer currently attached in Vienna or at headquarters. I replied that it was General Bronikowski, but added he was no longer on active service and was now just an advisor and friend to Poniatowski. He had served with Kosciuszko, but I didn't think he was familiar with modern infantry drill. I said there was an experienced officer in the Polish Guard Cavalry, Lieutenant Colonel Henryk Kaminski, who had served in the infantry. I know he had fallen out with General Krasinski and would readily leave the Guard. Also, I reminded the Emperor that there was staying in Vienna a Galician nobleman, who had served the Austrian Emperor but had recently been discharged for having divided loyalties. I said I knew this man, that his name was Krasicki and that he would be prepared to serve with us. So the Emperor ordered the chasseurs to bring out a table and some chairs from the post house, and had me get out the paper, ink, and quill which we always kept in our sabretaches. Then and there, at Stammersdorf on 7 July 1809, the Emperor dictated to me the decree establishing the 4th Regiment of the Legion of the Vistula (the first three were all in Spain), and appointed General Bronikowski Colonel-in-Chief, Lieutenant Colonel Henryk Kaminski Colonel in the field, and Lieutenant Krasicki commander of the first company. The regimental depot was to be Augsburg. Before long 3,000 deserters had collected there, and officers were sent from the Vistula Legion's main depot in Sedan to organize them.

After signing the decree the Emperor sent Fodoas off to fetch the rest of headquarters. When the service squadrons (which always marched with the Emperor) arrived, the Emperor mounted his horse and set off, alternately galloping and walking to let the service squadrons keep up. We reached Wolkersdorf, about two miles up the Brno road. There is a large castle there, where the main headquarters was set up when the staff reached it at about 2 P.M. The Guard made camp around it, and later in the day Marshal Davout's Corps passed by and pressed up on the Brno road. Marshal Massena's left wing marched to Stokerau. That day the Emperor made General Marmont a Marshal. He marched past us at the head of the Bavarians. The Emperor sent the Army of Italy to the river Marche, opposite Presburg, to confront Archduke John, who was only now marching to link up with Archduke Charles. He was three days too late. No doubt hearing of the Battle of Wagram, he halted on the river Marche.

The news reached the Emperor at Wolkersdorf that Massena had encountered Archduke Charles' main Austrian army, which was retreating from Stokerau to Znaim, and then to

Bohemia. Massena also reported that Rosenburg's corps, which had formed the left wing of the Austrian army at Wagram, was the only body retreating to Brno.[17] So the Emperor sent Marshal Davout after Rosenburg, with orders to march on Nicolsburg, and sent Marmont by back roads through Laa toward Znaim. He set off after him with the Guard. When the Emperor reached Laa, he sent me on ahead to join Marmont, who I found in a very good position above Znaim, from which direction he was under attack from Archduke Charles' whole army. For Marmont now stood astride the Austrian line of retreat, and from his position his artillery was firing into the Austrian columns retreating to Znaim. So Archduke Charles had been obliged to form up part of his army off the road and try to eject Marmont from his position. He would have definitely succeeded if one of Marmont's French divisions had not arrived in the nick of time to take the place of some particularly unsteady Bavarians. It had been raining heavily all day, which helped the Austrian attackers because the defenders' musketry was virtually ineffective, but the French division, which had accompanied Marmont from Illyria, held on bravely and would not concede the summit to the enemy. Marmont sent me back to the Emperor at Laa with a request for help. I forced my horse as hard as I could and was soon back with the Emperor, whom I found sitting in a hot bath to soothe a bad bout of croup. He told me to draw Marmont's position on paper; but when I began to draw Marmont's position and that of the Austrians for him, he said he knew the country and only wanted me to draw the positions of the two armies. Grabbing the pencil, he then soaked the paper and I could not draw on it any more. So he told me to go straight to Berthier and tell him to take the Guard without delay to Znaim. For my part, I was to change horses and return to Marmont to tell him the Guard was on the way.

When I got back to Marmont, I found him in the same position, with his French division in the front line and the Bavarians behind, except for one Bavarian brigade on the left wing in a less exposed position. The firing had already died down. The Austrians had stopped attacking and we could see their columns marching in close columns toward Znaim, and a great baggage train off the road to their left. The rain was still falling, but not as heavily as in the morning, so we could see the movements of Archduke Charles' entire army even more clearly than earlier. It was marching to Znaim in several tightly packed columns. Some of the cavalry had already passed Znaim and deployed facing us, against our right wing where there was a division of our light cavalry. The cavalry stood looking at each other but neither attempted a charge. The ground had been so soaked by the rain that it would have been difficult to charge across.

At about 4 P.M. we heard artillery fire on the opposite side of Znaim, on the road from Stokerau. It was Archduke Charles' rearguard, fighting Massena's advance guard in its approach to Znaim. Marshal Marmont immediately ordered the battery on highest ground to open fire, which had little effect on the Austrians, but alerted Massena that we were in the rear of the Austrian army.

At about 6 P.M. Berthier arrived with the light cavalry of the Guard. The Emperor also arrived in a carriage, alighted, and after examining the scene through his telescope for a few minutes, gave the order: "En avant!" The Illyrian division had begun its descent toward Znaim when a cavalry officer arrived with the news that Prince John Liechtenstein had approached our cavalry and asked them to tell Napoleon that the Austrian Emperor had sent

---

[17] The main French army was pursuing a single corps to Brno, while Massena alone was pursuing the main Austrian army.

him to parley. A quarter of an hour later Napoleon received him in his tent, which had been pitched on top of the hill among some beautiful cherry trees. After another fifteen minutes Berthier came out of the tent to order an immediate ceasefire.

Liechtenstein had been in the middle tent with Berthier and Napoleon, and the outer tent where the Staff waited was packed, with at least six generals present. When Liechtenstein passed from the middle to the outer tent he greeted each of our generals by name, and with great civility. He must have come across them in earlier campaigns. He then went off with Berthier to the latter's tent, about 100 paces away. On the other side stood another tent like Berthier's, and both were smaller versions of the Emperor's three room tent, which I have already described. The third tent was for the deputy chief of staff, General Monthion, who stood there with a crowd of staff officers. In Berthier's tent the armistice was signed. Only Berthier and Liechtenstein signed it. Several copies were made out on the spot and also signed, and orderly officers were sent off with them to all the detached corps. The Emperor gave me a copy to take to Archduke Charles' headquarters at Iglau, so he could arrange safe passage for me through Brno and Olomuniec to Krakow and Warsaw. The latest news from that front was that the Austrians had left Warsaw and were retreating on Sandomierz.

The armistice was signed on 12 July. The last article said: "The armies in Poland and Saxony will halt and remain where they are." But it was not specified whether they were to halt where they had been on the day the armistice was signed, that is 12 July, or where they would be on the day the news reached them. The Emperor told me to tell Prince Poniatowski that the reason he could not give the Poles what they wanted this time was because he dared not antagonize the Russians.[18] But he would remember the generous help provided by the Poles. As for the last article, he said: "If Prince Joseph has made a further advance since 12 July, let him interpret the article to mean both sides halt in the positions occupied on the day you arrive with the news. If, on the other hand, he has been forced to retreat, he should demand a return to the positions occupied on 12 July."

I set off with Septeuil, who had to take a copy of the armistice to the Saxon and Westphalian corps in Dresden. When we reached the Austrian lines, some infantry pickets on the edge of a wood cried out, "Wer da?" But Septeuil, who was very hot blooded, spurred his horse into a gallop, saying, "He'll never hit us!" My horse followed suit, and two infantrymen fired at us as we flew past. Further up the road were some more Austrians who heard the shots and obliged us to stop. Some general and his staff happened to be passing by, and when he stopped and recognized our uniforms, he ordered that we be allowed to pass. He sent over two of his staff to escort me, one a hussar and the other an ulan. They greeted us in fluent French, and one of them straight away asked after General Krasinski, Kozietulski, and a few officers in the Polish Guard. I asked why Poles should be of interest to him, and he replied that he and his brother were both Poles serving in the Austrian ulans, and that their name was Wojna. I was young and quick to anger in those days, and did not like to see Austrian trappings on a fellow countryman, so instead of answering his question, I declared: "You should be fighting on our side, not against us." I saw tears spring to his eyes. Yet he had done nothing wrong in serving Austria when his father's lands were under their rule. Young men should serve where they can, first to be active, and second to learn something. Perhaps I didn't understand that very well at that time.

---

18 The Poles wanted to restore Poland to full statehood. At no time in the Napoleonic Wars did the Emperor conclude that the benefit of restoring Poland would outweigh the negative impact on one or more of the three partitioning powers, Russia, Austria, and Prussia.

We went together to the Austrian headquarters. I told the Chief of Staff, General Wimpfen, who I was and where I was bound. He immediately wrote a laissezpasser instructing Rosenburg to let me through Brno and Olomuniec to Archduke Ferdinand's army. Septeuil left for Prague, while my road took me on from Znaim to Brno. In Znaim I hired a post-chaise and had reached Pohobitz by the following day. Not far from there I saw some of our cavalry scouts, and then some Austrian ones. A Hungarian hussar came down to the road from a nearby hill and stopped my carriage, then an n.c.o. who spoke German came along. After asking my business, he went to fetch his officer, who took me back to his quarters. This officer detailed another n.c.o. who accompanied me as far as Rosenburg's camp at Medryce. As we approached the last post house before Medryce, I could see from some way off that it was crowded with Austrian officers. So I ordered the carriage to halt, took out some Austrian coins, and asked the n.c.o. to be so kind as to hire a carriage for the next stage and to wake me when the new carriage was ready, as I was very tired and wanted to sleep in the old carriage while the new one was being prepared. I asked my driver to leave the old carriage outside the post house while he took a meal. I only pretended to sleep, as this was impossible in such a tiny iron box, from which the straw had fallen out, but I wanted to avoid having to tell all these officers yet again about the armistice. I had already been obliged to repeat my story to my escort, and to the officer commanding the cavalry outpost. But later on I still had to describe everything in even more detail to General Rosenburg, or perhaps it was his chief of staff as I didn't even ask to whom I had the honor of talking.

At last I reached Brno and was taken before the Governor, whose name was Lazanski but who told me he spoke no Polish.[19] He was at dinner, and invited me to join him. There were many officers around the table, and I was obliged yet again to recount the Battle of Znaim and events leading up to the armistice. Right after dinner a new post chaise was prepared. I set off again with an Austrian officer, as I had asked the Governor for a companion to help me on my way and avoid wasting further time explaining my business to every detachment commander met on the road. My companion was a most civil officer, a Monsieur Bredow, whom I got to know so well that when we reached the first post house, I could give him my purse and ask him to hire my next carriage and buy a drink for the postillion.

We reached Olomuniec at about midnight, to find the gates shut. M. Bredow went to find the sentry, but did not return for two hours, while I sat shivering in the carriage. He came back with a new carriage, which took another two hours to take us all round the city perimeter. I didn't know if my companion had been ordered to take this route before leaving Brno, or if the governor of Olomuniec was so simple minded as to be afraid to let one French officer pass through the town, and during the night at that, when I could not have seen anything.

Finally, at about 11 A.M. on 15 July we reached Wadowice, where Archduke Ferdinand had his headquarters. Ferdinand himself had arrived just before me, and I was invited to his quarters. An officer led the way. The Archduke read the armistice treaty; he invited me to lunch with him, asked my name, and said he was most unhappy to be fighting Poles, as he would far rather fight for justice for the Polish nation. "Much as I would have wished to fight the French, who invaded us, I had to face the Poles, whose cause is a just one. Anyway, I didn't succeed in Poland." The only other diner at lunch was Colonel Neuperg, who was standing in for the Chief of Staff, who was ill or had died. I had to recount again the Battle of Wagram, but not in such detail as he already knew something about it; but he had heard nothing of the

---

19 A number of Austrian noblemen were of Polish extraction, but no longer spoke the language.

fight at Znaim, so he questioned me closely on that engagement. Overall, Neuperg spoke more than the Archduke, and he seemed a bit of a braggart to me. The Archduke on the other hand was modest, honest, and beautifully mannered.

After we had eaten and I had answered all their questions, I wanted to be on my way. I asked for an orderly or an officer, or just a written laissezpasser, to let me through the Austrian lines so I could report in Krakow (the Archduke himself had told me earlier that Poniatowski had that day entered Krakow, either at the same time as the Russians or a little after them). But the Archduke would not answer and kept finding excuses not to release me, until finally I had to declare that the Emperor of France did not take kindly to his officers being prevented from doing their duty, even by hospitality. At this the Archduke explained that he could not permit me to travel any further, even though he had seen the signature of Archduke

ARCHDUKE FERDINAND

Charles, until an officer arrived from Charles' headquarters with the same orders to cease fire.

Four hours after my arrival an officer did finally arrive from Archduke Charles with the same document as mine, and straight away Archduke Ferdinand allowed me to leave. The officer who was to accompany me was already present, and a carriage had been ready to leave for two hours. When I took my leave, the Archduke said, "You see, sir, that I did not doubt you were telling the truth, as everything is prepared for your onward journey. But I could not let you go without orders from my commander. Please call to see me on your way back."

I set off immediately with my escorting officer. As we were leaving, two regiments of cuirassiers were just returning to camp on the left of town. They looked in superb condition. Behind them marched a regiment of hussars. I observed that the cuirassier regiments were under strength, and the hussars more numerous. The infantry had already made camp and lit fires. At Izdebnik we reached their forwardmost squadron of hussars. My companion reported to the officer on duty and soon we were permitted to pass through their picket line. Half an hour later, on our way to Mogilane, we saw peasants escorting two or three Austrian infantrymen, whom they had taken prisoner and disarmed, toward the Polish lines. We could also see some of our lancers on the high ground by Mogilane. I noticed that these sights ruffled my companion's nerves somewhat. Soon a lancer from our 6th regiment galloped up to our carriage; it was already growing dark, and I took off my greatcoat so that he could see my uniform. I intended to take leave of my companion there and let him return to the Austrian lines, but he asked if he could accompany me to Krakow and later return with me, if I did not mind. I readily agreed, assuming he also had permission from the Archduke. But when we arrived at Podgorze, Colonel Dziewanowski, who was garrison commander, would not let him into the town so we had to part there.

THE BALL AT THE GREAT HALL OF THE SUKIEUNICE

It is hard to describe my feelings as I drew nearer to Krakow, so recently liberated from foreign occupation. From the moment I passed the city gates at Podgorze I saw Polish soldiers everywhere, walking the streets arm in arm with the inhabitants. I was looking forward to seeing the Wielopolski family, to whom I was related on my mother's side.

When I got to the market square, which, like the rest of the city was brightly lit, I learned that Prince Poniatowski was attending a ball, laid on for him by the townspeople in the Great Hall at the Sukieunice [cloth merchant's hall]. I decided to go to his quarters at Krzysztopory and get one of his officers, whom I found there, to tell him I had arrived from the Emperor.

He came to see me immediately. For two hours I had to describe the battles of Wagram and Znaim, and he in turn told me about his advance on Krakow and occupation of the city that very day. Archduke Ferdinand had sent an envoy to ask for two day's grace, that is a 48 hour ceasefire, to permit him to evacuate the sick and his baggage train from Krakow. The Prince had readily agreed to this, welcoming the chance to save Krakow suffering, so he had halted for two days half a mile outside the city. After the two days were up (that is, on the day I arrived), the whole army was drawn up in parade uniform and set off for Krakow with the Prince and his staff at its head. But as they reached the Floryanska gate, they found it in the hands of some Russian cossacks who seemed determined to bar the Poles entry. For when Archduke Ferdinand was obliged to evacuate Krakow he had informed Prince Galicyn, who had marched with a corps of 30,000 men to Tarnow, ostensibly as Napoleon's ally. But in reality Prince Galicyn not only refused to fight the Austrians, but came to an open understanding with them.[20] So the Archduke, when he informed Galicyn that he was to leave Krakow, must have proposed that the Russians take his place. Galicyn had thereupon sent a light cavalry brigade and a cossack regiment by forced marches from Tarnow. Galicyn had earlier agreed with Poniatowski that the Polish army would operated on the left, and the Russians on the right bank of the Vistula. As a result of this agreement Poniatowski had evacuated Lwow, which his forces had already seized. So in entering Krakow,[21] the Russians broke the agreement with the Prince. When Poniatowski called upon the cossack commander at the gate to let him enter, the cossack refused, saying he had orders to bar the gate. At this the Prince drew his sword and charged with his staff right into the gateway among the cossacks. Our infantry followed at the double behind him and the cossacks were jammed along the sides of the arch. The Maryampolski hussar regiment was drawn up in the main square, but did not attempt to stop our army as it took over the town. The hussars stood back against the houses along one side of the square, and so bloodshed was avoided.

After our two hour interview the Prince went to rest in the next room, and with his permission I slept on a chaise longue in the ante-room for a good few hours. Early the next morning I reported to General Dabrowski, who was lodging with Lady Michalowska, of the Wielopolska family. I also met General Mielzynski there, who gave me a clean shirt to wear, as I had not had time to collect a change of clothes when I left Znaim. I also found Prince Henryk Lubomirski, whom I later accompanied to the houses of Lady Wielopolska, the dowager Lanckoronska and the Margrave Wielopolska. An officer came for me there from Prince Poniatowski, asking me to report immediately. I found him with Generals Fischer, Rozniecki, and Sokolnicki, as well as his staff officers. The Prince had received a letter that morning from Archduke Ferdinand, demanding that he leave Krakow because the armistice treaty had stipulated that all troops should remain in the positions occupied on the date of the signature, that is, on 12 July. The senior officers were in a quandary about what to do. The Prince decided to ask my opinion, as I had been present when the ceasefire agreement was signed, and should know better what the Emperor had in mind about how this article should be interpreted. I replied: "It seems to me that Krakow is such an important prize that the Prince cannot relinquish it without explicit instructions from the Emperor." I decided not to repeat what the Emperor had actually said, as he had not insisted I repeat it to the Prince, and I could see that Poniatowski was much less uncertain about what to do than his generals. He ordered straight away that the question be put in a letter to the Emperor, but when he remembered that the Archduke would not permit an officer of his to take the road to Olomuniec and Brno, he asked me if I would return immediately to the Emperor. I agreed to this, asking only that he make a copy of the ceasefire document for himself and send the original to Galicyn in Tarnow. I had no orders from the Emperor to do this, but if he had known about Galicyn's approach, he would certainly have sent an extra copy for the Russian. The Prince had a copy made straight away and sent his aide de camp off to Tarnow with the original.

They were just sitting down to dinner, but I excused myself and dined instead with my maternal aunt, Madame Wincentowa Wielopolska. One of the Prince's aides arranged for a

---

20 Galicyn's main objective was to protect Russian interests in the Polish territory seized after the partitions. Russia did not welcome Poniatowski's success in taking back so much of Austrian Poland, as they knew the Poles, having recovered their plundered provinces from Prussia and Austria, would hope then to recover the lands that Russia had annexed.
21 Which is on the left bank of the Vistula.

horse and trap to collect me there. I left at about 3 p.m., and by 8 was back with Archduke Ferdinand.

On the road I passed Austrian troops encamped between Izdebnik and Wadowice, which meant they had already begun marching on Krakow. I told the Archduke that if he wanted

NEIPPERG

to enter the city, Prince Poniatowski would defend it and moreover would be supported by the entire population, who would fight hard to protect their homes. They had welcomed the Polish army so completely that I did not doubt they would rally to its support. Anyway, if it came to a fight the only quarter to be contested was Podgorze, because the Archduke would get no further; if the worst came to the worst and the Austrians captured this suburb, the Poles would undoubtedly blow up the Vistula bridge.[22] I added that I also thought there could be a battle on the right bank, as Prince Poniatowski considered his agreement with Galicyn to have been broken by the Russians crossing into Krakow, and Poniatowski would therefore not hesitate to cross to the right bank. Furthermore, I was carrying a letter to the Emperor from the Prince asking if he should really abandon Krakow and saying he would not do so without an explicit order. The Archduke did not seem too perturbed by what I said, but I could see Neuperg was seething with rage.

After half an hour with the Archduke, another carriage arrived from the post house and I went on my way. At Olomuniec I was again forced to wait two hours at the guard house outside the city fortifications. An officer finally arrived with a change of carriage and once again I was taken all around the perimeter of the town. This time it was broad daylight, so if anybody had wanted to learn the state of the city's fortifications, they had a far better chance of doing so by traveling round the perimeter than by passing straight through the middle of town. The officer who accompanied me admitted that the consequences of this precaution had not been thought through. Anyway, Olomuniec was such an old fortress that the Emperor, who had passed this way in 1805, would undoubtedly have a detailed map already.

At the last post house at Stammersdorf there was no carriage available but I didn't mind, as I had no baggage with me. I covered the last stretch on horseback, crossing the Danube, passing through Vienna, and finally arriving at Schoenbrunn.

22 Podgorze is on the right bank of the river and the rest of the city on the left.

"Where is the Polish Army?" asked the Emperor.

"In Krakow."

"Oh, how your motherland must rejoice!"

That was our first exchange on my return. Then he asked me for all the details, and when I told him a Russian brigade had entered Krakow, he turned all his questions to Galicyn and his army. I had to confess that I had not visited Galicyn, and had only sent the ceasefire document by the hand of another officer. At that he became very angry and ordered me to my quarters, several times repeating: "When I send an officer on an errand, I expect him to investigate everything, and I mean everything, around him. And you must have guessed how interested I would be in the state of a Russian corps."

I retired in confusion upstairs. I was so tired that I fell asleep right away. It was only 10 A.M. on the following morning when a colleague came to call me for breakfast that I remembered that I was under arrest. I asked him to find out from General Savary, standing in for Caulaincourt, who was responsible for our administration, whether I was under open arrest or close arrest. General Savary asked the Emperor and soon my colleague Talhouet arrived to tell me the Emperor had pardoned me. Open arrest would have meant keeping my weapons and only leaving my quarters for meals. But under close arrest, I would have had to relinquish my sword and been confined to my quarters twenty four hours a day.

I had eaten very little on the road. But when I got back to Schoenbrunn I still couldn't eat, as I had great difficulty swallowing. I think several months of eating irregular and often cold meals on the move had weakened my stomach. I had to consult Iwan, the Emperor's personal physician. He concluded that both my stomach and my lungs had been weakened. He instructed me to drink camomile tea before every meal, and later, when my stomach had settled, to take a cure of asses milk. This I did after peace was concluded and we were back in Paris.

We spent four more weeks in Schoenbrunn while the peace treaty was negotiated. Life was a bit repetitive. The most exciting incident during this time was the attempt on the Emperor's life by a German student, who wasn't even Austrian. He had come from north Germany to Schoenbrunn for this purpose. He pushed his way through the crowds that were allowed to gather every day to watch the parades in front of the palace. A Gendarme of the Guard caught him just as he broke from the crowd and ran toward the Emperor with his right hand hidden in his coat. They found a long knife on him, and the student admitted he wanted to kill the Emperor as the tyrant of Germany. He was shot, or perhaps he was hanged, a few days later.

We returned to Paris. After six weeks I regained my health completely and went to join the Emperor at Rambouillet. He was staying there after his separation from the Empress Josephine and his decision to marry again, in the hope of giving France an heir to the throne.

There were two of us on duty at Rambouillet. One day the Emperor called us both to him, and to me he said: "I am sending you on a mission to St. Petersburg," and to Fodoas he said, "You are going to Madrid." It seemed odd to me that the Emperor should send me to Russia and I ventured to ask: "You wish to send me, Sire, a Pole, to St. Petersburg?"

"You're right," he replied, "so you go to my brother in Madrid."[23]

With that he handed me a set of orders which his secretary, Fain, had written out, ordering our names to be swapped over. Then he gave me some further instructions orally.

---

23 The Russians would have taken the arrival of a Polish officer as a deliberate insult.

THE VISTULA LANCERS AT OCANA

I went to Paris for my things, as my errand wasn't urgent, but I still set off that night. From each camp I passed through, at Bayonne, Vittoria, Burgos, and Madrid, I sent a report addressed personally to the Emperor describing the strength of our armies. I told King Joseph that the Emperor would not now arrive in person, but that he wished the army to take the field, as the Spanish army was advancing on Madrid. As it happened, it had already been defeated at Ocana. The Polish division, consisting of the 2nd, 7th, and 9th infantry regiments of the Duchy of Warsaw, had played an important part in that battle. The colonels of these regiments were Potocki, Sobolewski, and Sulkowski. Konopski's lancer regiment had fallen on the retreating Spanish infantry from behind. I don't know if this regiment alone bagged so many prisoners, or whether it was given the task of escorting all the prisoners taken in the battle, but a detachment of Konopski's horse brought back nearly 10,000 of them from Ocana to Madrid.

When I returned to Paris I found that the Emperor had moved from the capital to Compiegne, where he was awaiting the arrival of her Highness Marie Louise, whose hand Berthier had taken in the Emperor's name at the Austrian border, and who Berthier was

PRINCE SCHWARZENBURG'S BALL

bringing to Compiegne in the company of Queen Caroline Murat of Naples. I was on duty throughout this period.

A week after Marie Louise's arrival at Compiegne, the ceremonial wedding took place in Paris in the gallery of the Louvre. There was a lot of pomp and ceremony. The train of the young Empress's dress was carried by royal ladies: the Queens of Spain, Naples, Holland, and Westphalia[24]; the daughter of the King of Wurtemburg, the vicereine of Italy, the daughter of the king of Bavaria, and Eliza Baccioli, the Emperor's oldest sister.

All the Kings and Princes of the Rhine Confederation were also in Paris, as well as the King of Saxony (our own Duke of Warsaw), who was the most distinguished of all. Balls were held daily at the Imperial Palace or at one of the other of the great houses. The Austrian Ambassador, Prince Schwarzenburg, had a pavilion constructed in his garden which was fabulously decked out. His reception began at 11 P.M., but about midnight the gauze netting which was draped around the pavilion caught fire and soon the whole place was ablaze.

---

24 This assemblage of queens was not so impressive as it sounds: the queens were respectively Napoleon's sister-in-law, sister, step-daughter, and sister-in-law, all queens appointed by Napoleon himself and imposed on their countries.

Prince Schwarzenburg and his aides surrounded the Emperor and Empress and shepherded them to safety, but the guests, pressing to get out, fell over each other, and a few ladies, as well as the Russian envoy, Prince Kurakin, were badly hurt. Princess Schwarzenburg died immediately, and over the coming week many more also lost their lives.

Prince Kurakin had been a very wealthy Russian magnate. He had certainly been appointed because he could afford the cost of being Ambassador. The real work was done by Neselrode, whom I saw almost every night in society. He was usually accompanied by his colleague Krudener, son of the famous Lady Krudener, and by Boutiakin and Ukrainiec. I got to know these last two very well. They were all atypical Russians: they had a sober and healthy outlook on the world. I also got to know the Embassy's Pope.[25] I'm not sure he was a great theologian, but he was a fine fellow. I studied Russian with him, taking lessons three times a week. That was the one and only time in my life that I kept frequent company with Russians. I took the opportunity to learn their language because I thought this would help me in the war which everyone was already expecting.

A month after the wedding, the Emperor promoted all of us orderly officers to lieutenant colonel and allocated us to regiments. I was assigned to the Polish Lancers of the Guard. We retained the privileges that we had enjoyed as orderly officers, which meant that we could enter his chambers in the mornings when he gave out his orders for the day. So having received my appointment to the Guard, I went to see him the following day and asked if he would place me instead in Konopski's lancer regiment.[26] The Emperor asked me why, and I replied that Konopski's lancers were on active service while the Guard regiment was at Chantilly. The Emperor said: "The Guard will be fighting as well before, long, and I don't want you too far away from me." He would not change his mind, so I had to thank him for my new post and set off for Chantilly. Throughout my time there General Krasinski [the commander of the Guard regiment] was very kind to me.

In Chantilly, we lieutenant colonels were on duty on a weekly rota. At the time, there were only two of us, Kozietulski and I, as Tomasz Lubienski had been sent to Sedan to form a new regiment of Polish lancers, which became the 8th regiment in the French army, and Stokowski had been give Konopski's regiment when the latter was made a general. The Emperor had transformed six dragoon regiments into lancers, so Konopski's old regiment became the 7th, and Lubienski's new formation became the 8th.

I used to serve one week in Chantilly, then a week in Paris. Sometimes during the winter of 1810—11, Kozietulski would stand in for me during my week so I could stay longer in Paris. I used to stay with some friends of mine, the Caramans, with whom I kept my horse and equipment so that when the regiment came to Paris for parades, I used only to ride out to meet them at the city gates, then march back into the city with them. Thus passed the winter of 1810 —11, but when spring came and the regiment resumed training, I stayed full time at Chantilly.

In spring 1811 I was ordered to take 150 of our lancers and 150 Guard chasseurs to Boulogne, where the Emperor was to make a visit. He arrived soon after us. There was one division there, in the same camp which the whole army had occupied in 1804 preparing for the invasion of England, and from which it had set off for Ulm, Austerlitz, and later, Jena in 1806. There were also a few hundred barges still at Boulogne, which had been collected to transport the army to England.

25 Pope was a title sometimes used for Russian Orthodox priests.
26 The 1st Regiment, Vistula Lancers.

NAPOLEON AND HIS NEW EMPRESS

The Emperor had the division put through its paces, then went on board one of the boats. I was detailed to bring along fifty chasseurs, and the whole flotilla put to sea. The weather was quite calm all morning, and our oarsmen had an easy job of it. But around noon a west wind sprang up and three English ships appeared: a frigate and two brigs. They were in full sail and made such good speed for Boulogne that they got there before the last boats and captured two of them, with forty occupants apiece. By that time we had got the Emperor back on to dry land, for as soon as the frigate appeared, our vice admiral had ordered us to return to port.

From Boulogne only twenty five horsemen escorted the Emperor to Flushing. There were fourteen ships of the line and four frigates in the port. The Emperor spent the night in one of the ships, the City of Warsaw. The next day he inspected all the vessels, and after lunch went on to Antwerp. The rest of us arrived two days later, then after another two days we again set off ahead of him for Amsterdam.

Kozietulski then arrived with his detachment, which I joined up with at Utrecht. As senior officer, he took over command of the escort.

From Amsterdam, the Emperor went with a squadron each of lancers and chasseurs to explore the coastline as far as Texel and Helder, then returned to Amsterdam. From there we again set off ahead of him to Nijmegen and Dusseldorf, and after a few days there he returned to Paris. We also went back, by way of Akwizgran and Liege. Except in Boulogne, he had been accompanied on this journey by the Empress, who had joined him in Antwerp.

I spent the winter of 1811 — 12 much as I had the previous year. There was a lot of talk about war with Russia, but it was only in May that any decision was made and we marched off by way of Reims, Verdun, Moguncya [Mainz], Dresden, and Glogau, to Poznan.

THE WAR OF 1812

THE WINTER BEFORE THE CAMPAIGN

We spent the winter of 1811 - 12 very happily in Paris. By all accounts, the Emperor decided on his return from Holland to provide entertainment for his much younger bride, and so every day there was a reception or ball, sometimes in the Tuileries, sometimes at the house of one of his sisters or Queen Hortense, who retained the title, "Queen of Holland," even though Holland had been incorporated into France, and its royal family abolished by an unaccountable decision of the Emperor. I say unaccountable, for how could he expect people to show respect for monarchs which he created one day, only to unseat or transfer to another throne the next, as if they were mere functionaries?[1]

Besides the balls hosted by the Imperial family, there were receptions at the houses of all the Ministers and Foreign Ambassadors, including that of the Russian, Prince Kurakin, even though there was growing talk of war with Moscow. The problem was that the Emperor Alexander either refused, or was unable to fulfil his obligations under the Treaty of Erfurt to close Russian ports to trade with England. As I have mentioned, I knew some of Kurakin's deputation. Prince Kurakin, a very wealthy boyar, was just the figurehead. The real brain of the Embassy was Nesselrode, whom I used to see nearly every day in select and exclusive company. He saw things very clearly and explained that Russia could not survive without trade with the English, and that it was beyond Alexander's power to close it down completely. Another deputy was Buriakin, who was younger than Nesselrode and became good friends with me. He assured me he was from an old Lithuanian family, and that his parents had land in the Ukraine and considered themselves more Polish than Russian. I also made friends with young Krudener. He was the son of the famous Madame Krudener, the Protestant evangelist who later came to exercise great influence over Alexander. I mustn't forget to mention Czerniszew, as he caused a great fuss at the time when he "bought" two poor secretaries from the Ministry of War, who gave him strength returns for all the Corps in the French army. Czerniszew departed with the information so rapidly that the order to arrest him sent by the telegraph still arrived at the frontier after his escape.[2] This incident left a sad and depressing memory with those of us who had seen him once, at Aspern in 1809, when as an officer on attachment he had stood in the thick of the firing.

Finally, to complete my description of the Russian delegation, I should mention their pope, who came three times weekly to my quarters to give me Russian lessons. In selecting popes for service abroad, the Muscovites must only have chosen the men with the most sober bearing. He had a good natural wit but not learning, and all in all was somewhat limited as a human being.

Finally, in April, war with Russia seemed certain. We left our barracks in Chantilly in early May and marched to Reims, then Verdun. There our Polish officers became very friendly with some Englishmen who were on a private tour of the continent, and these men said they wanted France to defeat Russia so that our country could be recreated. I met there a Lord Blanchy, a Lord Bogle, and some of their company.

---

1 Chlapowski's concern was understandable: Polish hopes for a return to national sovereignty were strained by the frequent examples of Napoleon's disregard for the rights of small nations. But even his brand of patronage was better than none.
2 At this time, the telegraph was a series of semaphore towers.

From Verdun we made for Longwy and the Luxembourg, which is a very strong fortress with a large garrison. General Konopka joined us there. We then passed through some beautiful country. The views around Trier in particular were fabulous. I left the regiment at Moguncya and took a post chaise to Dresden. There I collected my sister and together we visited my father at Turwa, where we spent ten days. I rejoined my regiment at Glogau and we marched to Wschowe. While we were there I took all the regimental staff and officers to see my father, and we danced all night.

In early June we reached Poznan. It seemed too late in the season to start a war with Russia that year, especially as the corps of the Grand Army had only just started mobilizing. A Prussian corps was forming on the Baltic, and was to form the left wing of the army, while an Austrian corps was to form the right wing. It was clear from the delay in collecting his forces and from the disposition of his troops that the Emperor wished only to intimidate Alexander and his Muscovites, threatening their 200,000 men with 400,000. That must explain why he put the Austrians and the Prussians on the wings, for he must have known he could not count on their whole hearted cooperation in the war. Had he been seeking or expecting war, he would surely have placed them in the middle among the French and Polish armies.

When we reached Vilnius, it was more clear than ever that the Emperor did not want war. He kept negotiating non-stop with Alexander. In Vilnius we were idle for two weeks. Only when the Emperor finally realized that the Emperor Alexander would not sign a treaty on his terms did he find himself obliged to go to war and invade Russia so late in the year.

After this introduction, let us return to Poznan.

The Campaign

The whole Guard was camped at Poznan. Of our brigade, the Chasseurs à Cheval were in Owinskie, and we[3] were in Murowana Goslina. We attended various receptions in the neighboring country, one of them at my aunt's in Lopuchow. While we were in Poznan I was ordered to take 300 cavalrymen, 150 chasseurs à cheval and 150 Polish lancers, to set off ahead of the Emperor and post detachments along the route from Torun to Gdansk. I set off immediately. On the first day we stopped at Gniezno, on the second beyond Mogilin, and on the third two miles beyond Inowroclaw. Here, most of my detachment was quartered in villages by the road for the night. My captain and I, together with two officers and one platoon, were allocated Kaczkowo, where there was a palace but virtually no village. When we reached the palace gate I found the billeting officer waiting for me. He told me a Wurtemburg major and five officers were installed in the palace, that their infantry company was billeted in the outbuildings, and they had no intention of letting us in. I led my men into the courtyard, brushing aside two Wurtemburgers on guard at the gate who tried to bar our path. I dismounted and ordered my platoon to do the same. Then I went into the palace and found the Wurtemburg officers in a downstairs room. Their badges of rank used to be higher than their real station, so that a "major" was equivalent to a captain in other armies. I knew about this quirk, and addressing the officer wearing major's epaulettes as captain, I explained politely that we were travelling by forced marches to place outposts along the Emperor's route, that at 3 A.M. the next day we would go on our way, and that our horses needed rest. Would he kindly remove his horses from the stables for one night so that ours could take their

3   The Polish Lancers of the Guard

place? He did not even stand up to speak to me, but answered frostily that he would not do as I asked. "In that case captain," I said, "you had better send some soldiers to catch the horses, because I am going to have them turned out of the stables anyway."

I went outside and ordered some of my soldiers to do as I had threatened. Then, having learnt from the billeting officer that the lady of the manor, Madame Dambska, was upstairs, I went in search of her. I found her with her daughter in a salon in the furthest corner of the house. She greeted me gracefully, saying: "How can I offer you hospitality, sir, when these Wurtemburgers have taken over all our stoves and their soldiers are cooking their food downstairs, while our servants have to smuggle bread upstairs to us. I still have a little coffee and tea with me. We have been living like this for five days, and I am in constant fear of fire because they are lighting cooking fires all over the place."

I calmed these ladies down as well as I could. I had my cook with me, who had

THE POLISH LANCERS CROSS THE RIVER WILIA

a pack horse loaded with provisions and had bought meat and bread in Inowroclaw. I invited my two ladies to be my guests at dinner.

Shortly afterwards, Lieutenant Lubanski came in to report that when our men had turned out the Wurtemburg horses and installed our own, a few Wurtemburgers had climbed on the thatched roof of the stable and began making loopholes through the straw. One of our chevaulegers had gone up after them and thrown one of them off the roof. This fellow had fallen onto the flagstones in front of the stable and had made such a noise with his howling that their captain had rushed outside with his sword drawn and fallen upon our chevauleger. Finally sergeant major Smolski, who had been distributing fodder in the stable, came up to the captain, wrenched the sword from the man's hand, and broke it over his knee, saying in German: "Find another use for this toy!" Whereupon the captain retreated in shame to the house and did not show his face again.

After this incident I feared that the Wurtemburgers might exact revenge on the ladies of the house after we left, or set light to the place. Passing through Inowroclaw I had seen that some French cuirassiers were stationed there, under the command of General Sebastiani. So I wrote a letter to him straight away describing the Wurtemburgers' behavior and our scuffle with them, and asking him to send a squadron here before 3 A.M. to billet in the palace and protect the inhabitants from harm.

Madame Dambska and her daughter had not left their room for five days, and I was permitted to escort her daughter on a walk around the grounds. Everywhere the Wurtemburgers had erected shelters under the trees, lit fires, and were cooking their delicacies. Smoke hung in the air all around us. It was no better in the room where their officers lived. Indoors and out, I could smell similar odors and the same grimy smoke which comes from cooking with a lot of fat.

Madame Dambska's chef appeared, and he and my cook prepared supper for us. We had just sat down to eat at about 9 P.M. when into the room came Sebastiani's a.d.c., Lavoistine. It was less than four hours since I had sent my letter. Lavoistine was a young, cheerful officer whom I had known in Paris. He had been in such a hurry that he had taken one hour to cover the two miles from Inowroclaw. He told me from General Sebastiani that a squadron of cuirassiers would arrive in Kaczkowa before 3 A.M. to make sure the Wurtemburgers did no damage. Sebastiani had also sent a report to Marshal Ney, to whose corps they belonged. Lavoistine's horse was exhausted, so he stayed the night with us. We stayed up until midnight and Madame Dambska entirely forgot her fear in the cheerful company of Lavoistine.

Having confirmed that the cuirassiers were on their way, I called together the dozen or so local peasants who were in Kaczkowo, some of whom had refused to leave the wagons and horses that the Wurtemburgers had seized, and others who had been forced to chop wood and generally do their bidding. I told these men to go to all the villages from which the Wurtemburgers had stolen horses and cattle and to tell the owners to report to Kaczkowa by 3 A.M. when their possessions would be returned to them.

When we had taken our leave of the ladies, we tried to sleep for two hours, but long before dawn the sound of trumpets back down the road announced that the rest of my detachment and the cuirassier squadron were approaching. During the night the local peasants had gathered, and each was already waiting by his possessions. Before I had even called my men to horse, the peasants had scattered in all directions, taking their wagons and livestock. The cuirassier captain rode up to me and said: "Rest assured, sir, that I will allow nothing bad to happen here." He then uttered some epithets about Wurtemburgers that I need not repeat.[4]

We set off for Torun. We didn't stop to feed our horses until Chelmzo. By nightfall we were in Grudziadz. The countryside was completely flat, so we marched almost non-stop at the trot. The Guard cavalry nearly always rode at the trot when the road was level, and even when it inclined a little. But we always went downhill at a walk, and often dismounted and led our horses. Our normal routine on the march would be to walk for the first hour, then stop for ten minutes to dismount, give our horses a drink, and tighten all their saddle straps. After an hour's march every horse loses some weight off its stomach and the straps loosen, so it is a good idea to tighten them. We would then remount and walk on for a few hundred paces, then break into a trot if the ground allowed it and continue thus for two solid hours. By this method we were able to march twice the distance normally covered by cavalry. When a few squadrons were in column of route, we used to keep a gap of at least a hundred paces between squadrons while trotting, so that everyone could ride as if he were travelling alone, by keeping a steady pace and not having to stop at any time. By marching at a trot not only do you save time, but the soldiers don't get so sleepy as when marching at a walk. When a rider does begin to drop off, the rhythm of his horse jerks him awake.

4 The Wurtemburg contingent was notorious throughout the Guard Army for its lack of discipline or respect for the local populace. In an age and army where neither quality was plentiful, this was no mean feat.

Before we reached our day's destination, our quartermaster would distribute billeting cards while we were still on the march so that every soldier could go straight to his lodging and none had to retrace his steps. We had a similar system in the mornings when we would all muster at a spot in front of the place we had spent the night, and in the direction of our intended route. Again, this meant no one had to retrace his steps. You can't do this with young soldiers. With them you have to march to a designated spot, hand out billeting cards there and instruct them to return to that same spot the following morning. But as all our men were experienced in the Guard, we could let them go off on their own and always rely on them to report to the right place next day. It is self evident that by marching in the way I have described, both horses and men are spared as much as possible from fatigue, as each only covers as much of the road as a single horseman would have to travel.

We reached Grudziadz [Graudenz] an hour before nightfall. I took off my uniform, put on my surtout and forage cap, and set off for the fort.[5] A French light infantry officer had quarters nearby, and together we went to have a look at the fortifications by the city gate, on the Vistula river. When we reached the glacis we found two soldiers on guard who did not want to let us in. One of them called his sergeant who came right over and explained that we could only enter by permission of the commandant. I told him who I was and asked him to convey to the commandant my request that we be permitted entry. Five minutes later we heard drums being beaten and the colonel commandant appeared with another officer. I noticed he was surprised to see us wearing surtouts and forage caps for he was in full dress uniform complete with sword. But he invited us to come in and look wherever we wished. When we passed through the outer gate the sentries presented arms, and on top of that we saw the whole garrison drawn up on the drill square. When I asked what they were doing there, the commandant replied that there was an absolute standing order that the garrison had to turn out in full uniform whenever a staff officer paid a visit, unless that officer gave express orders to the contrary. I apologized profusely that we had come in undress uniform and without our swords, and explained that we had thought we could enter the fort without formality during peacetime. The next day I donned my parade uniform and went with one of my officers to pay a proper call on the commandant: he was obviously very pleased to receive us and was very polite.

The fort at Grudziadz forms a semi-circle with its base on the Vistula. There are three bastions and two half-bastions all linked by earthworks. Together they make a fort in the style of Montalembert. There are more earthworks nearer the town. They are all very well constructed, with excellent firing platforms. All this makes Grudziadz a very strong fortress, which totally dominates the Vistula.

On the 3rd I was in Kwidzyn, where I met some Prussian acquaintances. On the 6th I escorted the Emperor to Sztum. I then returned to Kwidzyn, where only one of my platoons remained. The other four under my command had been sent to Malborg, Tczew, Pruszcz, and Gdansk. Each of them had orders to rejoin me at Kwidzyn after the Emperor had passed on his way from Torun to Gdansk.

The main body of our regiment had marched from Torun straight to Gambin. My detachment caught up with it a few miles short of Kowno, just when the Emperor arrived from Konigsburg on his way to the crossing over the Niemen. The next day he crossed the bridge

5 This was the undress uniform, worn when off duty.

NAPOLEON AND THE POLISH LANCERS ENTER RUSSIA
FROM THE COLLECTION OF RONALD AKSNOWICZ

with us behind him. Kozietulski was officer in command that day and the Emperor ordered him to cross the river Wilia to chase off some cossacks who had collected on the far bank. Our boys jumped into the water and some were drowned, but the cossacks disappeared. The Emperor ordered General Konopka, who was our grosmajor, or senior field officer, to follow Kozietulski over with three squadrons and conduct a reconnaissance as far as Czerwony Dwor on the river Niewiaza. Off we went, and at Czerwony Dwor we were greeted by M. Zabiello and his daughter, who spent the evening with us in bivouac. We had crossed the Wilia at a ford only a dozen or so paces from the spot Kozietulski had swum across. Our saddlecloths had hardly even got wet, and the water had only reached our horses' bellies.

During the night we returned to Kovno. The Emperor had gone off to join the advance guard on the Vilnius road. The next day we set off after him and within two marches were in Vilnius. I spent a week on duty there. Every day the Emperor went off to see some attraction in the city, and meanwhile his troops were marching toward Dzwina. The rumor was that part of the Russian army had retired behind Dzwina, that they had made camp at Dryssa and that they Emperor Alexander intended to make a stand there on the old frontier of Russia. The rest of the Russian army under Bagration was retiring on Minsk and the Dnieper. The King of Westphalia was following Bagration, but he paused in his pursuit in disobedience to the Emperor's instructions, and was banished to Cassel; his command went to Davout.

In Vilnius Count Pac gave a ball for the Emperor in his palace. The Tyzenhauz family also lived there.[6]

Although we had a good time in Vilnius, news reached us there of the hardships and terrors of war, inflicted on the populace by the indiscipline and savagery of our army. My heart bled to see my country suffer so.

I used often to visit Countess Gedroic. There I meet an old flame of mine, Mademoiselle Zxolia Tyzenhauz. I also met this lady at the house of Madame Kossakowska, a Potocka by birth. I had never expected to be in Vilnius for so long. The conduct of both sides in this campaign was a mystery to me.

A deputation came from the Sejm in Warsaw to ask the Emperor to announce the union of Lithuania and the Duchy of Warsaw. The Emperor gave an ambiguous reply which saddened many of us deeply. Our only hope was that developments in the war would oblige the Emperor to do as we asked. The Emperor obviously still wanted to appease Russia and ally himself with her against England. He could not therefore rebuild Poland because once Moscow lost her Polish provinces she would have nothing more to lose and, with British help, would refuse to make peace and would fight until the bitter end. The Emperor would then find himself at war at both ends of Europe, in Spain and in Poland. That way he could never bring England to heel. We were no more than a useful pawn in his game. I thought often of the words of our old commander-in-chief, Kosciuszko, and in particular his advice: "Learn at the feet of the greatest warrior of the Age."

From Vilnius we eventually marched off with the Emperor to Glebokie on the Vitebsk road. A few miles short of this city there was a bloody skirmish at Ostrowna between Murat's advance guard and the Russian rearguard. One of our squadrons, which was escorting Murat in person, lost heavily on this occasion as the King of Naples cared as little for his own safety as for that of anybody else. When we arrived on the scene with the Emperor, the cannon, which had been firing for hours, were now silent. Murat's cavalry must have been tired out as the Emperor sent our Guard brigade forward in their place. But the Muscovites must have suffered badly as well because as we approached Vitebsk we came several times upon their rearguard of cossacks and Russian Guard hussars, but they never once stood to fight. All they did each time was send out flankers to harry us, while their main body retired. We caught a few red cossacks. They are a very tall and powerful race.[8]

By the time we entered Vitebsk, the enemy had deserted the city. They had retreated across the Dzwina and were on the road to Wielkie Lukie, that is, the St. Petersburg road. They had not destroyed the bridge on the Dzwina, as there was no point. The river was fordable in places, and a bridge could easily have been rebuilt using material from the forest and nearby huts. At the first village we came to, we discovered the main Russian army had left the St. Petersburg road, and turned right onto the Smolensk road. Meanwhile, Bagration's corps, retreating before Davout, had crossed the Dnieper below Roghaczew, where its rearguard had put up a stout defence against Davout and held his advance guard long enough for their entire army to cross the river in safety.

6 The Tyzenhauz were family friends of the Chlapowski's who had helped the author after his release from Russian prison in 1807 (see chapter 1)
7 i.e. of Polish Guard Lancers
8 These Russians appear to have been the 2nd Brigade of the Guard Division, which contained the Russian Life Guard Hussars and the Lifeguard Cossacks. The latter's uniform was scarlet, unlike ordinary cossacks who generally wore dark blue. The description of their stature also fits that of Guardsmen.

LANCER PROVIDING A GUIDE TO NAPOLEON

COSSACKS

By his forced marches from Kowno to Vilnius, and then from Vilnius to Vitebsk, the Emperor had succeeded in dividing the Russian army into two bodies; Barclay de Tolly with the Tsar retiring to Dryssa on the river Dzwina, and Bagration retreating to Minsk and the Dnieper. The Emperor concluded that neither enemy would dare stand and face him alone, so he decided to allow the two bodies time to join up. He obviously guessed that Barclay de Tolly, marching from Vitebsk to Smolensk, and Bagration marching from Roghaczew to Mscislaw, were seeking to link up again. While we gave them the time to do so, our army spread out around the towns and villages near Vitebsk and rested.

Eventually, the Emperor received firm confirmation that Bagration had rejoined the main Russian army, and we in turn set off from Vitebsk to the Dnieper where we were to join Davout. He had the Polish corps under his command. We crossed the Dnieper at Dabrowna. The Dnieper changes direction several times on the way to Smolensk, the largest bend in the river being near Katane. News reached the headquarters at Dabrowna that a Russian force had crossed the Dnieper to our side and was at Katane, threatening our left flank. The Emperor sent four squadrons of Polish Guards [from the total of six] under Kozietulski to investigate. We set off after midnight, and with the help of two old peasants, who incidentally could still speak Polish, arrived at a spot half a mile from Katane. There we encountered our first cossacks. Our main body halted by some buildings and one squadron went out to meet them. The cossacks retreated off to our left, toward the Dnieper. At about this time the sun rose and we were able to see the country round about. To our front stood a line of cavalry on the crest of a hill, screened by a few hundred cossacks. Kozietulski now recalled the first platoon, which had already come to grips with the cossacks, and he formed the leading squadron into line. The regular cavalry must have been able to see our other three squadrons in support, as they did not move from their position. But the cossacks approached with increasing boldness, firing with their ancient pistols. As we sent nobody out to skirmish with them, they came closer and closer, shouting: "Lachy!"[9] when they discovered we were Polish. A cossack officer on a fine grey came as close as a hundred paces, perhaps less, and in good Polish challenged us to meet him in single combat. Kozietulski forbade any of us to move. The cossack jumped from his horse and cried: "Now you can catch me!" He then took off his cap and waved it in the air, then having concluded that he would not provoke us, he leapt on his horse and rejoined his men. The cossacks must have fired a hundred shots at us, but not one hit its target. Cossacks will not charge even a lone squadron if is in good order. They like best to tackle individuals, whom they taunt in order to lure them out of the way, entrap them, and take them prisoner. For that reason you should never let impetuous, bold, or excitable troopers go out and skirmish with cossacks.

As it grew lighter, we could see a great column of enemy cavalry on the far side of the Dnieper, marching toward Smolensk. Soon the cossacks, and the hussars who had been on the hill, formed column and followed them away. We returned to Dabrowna. The Emperor had expected the enemy to offer battle near Dabrowna, Lady, or Krasnie, but now concluded that Barclay de Tolly and Bagration would not link up until Smolensk. All this happened on 15 August, which was the Emperor's name day, and he had wanted a battle that day.

So we went on past Lady and Krasnie, and arrived before Smolensk. One and a half miles in front of the town, near Mscislaw, we were joined by Poniatowski's Polish Corps, which was acting as advance guard for Davout. I was most impressed by the appearance of Prince Sulkowski's cavalry division. They had a good soldierly appearance and their horses were magnificent. That first day I saw only the first brigade. This consisted of Tolinski's "Silver" Hussars, so named to differentiate them from Uminski's regiment which had the same uniform but with gold buttons and lace, and the 5th Chevaulegers, who were very fine and even better mounted than the Hussars.

Smolensk is on the left bank of the Dnieper. Our army deployed to face it, with the Polish V Corps on the right flank. The Emperor's tents had been pitched right in the front line, with the guard camped behind. From the Emperor's tent we could see all of Smolensk, with its walls and towers, on which we could make out Russian infantry and cannon. There were masses of cossacks circling in front of the city. Between the French line and the city walls was a massive gully into which the cossacks had spilled. As I was on duty that day, I was ordered by the Emperor to take a squadron and force the cossacks from the gully so that he could inspect the enemy fortifications close to. He mounted his horse and followed close behind us. As soon as we entered the gully, the cossacks withdrew. Coming up out of the ditch on the far side, I deployed the squadron in a single line, as I expected the enemy to shoot at us from the walls. Sure enough, they fired a number of howitzer shells, one of which exploded in the middle of the squadron. A few men were wounded, and some horses broke ranks in fright, so the cossacks seized the moment to charge us. They were upon us very quickly, and I had to parry one of their lances with my sword. I damaged the lance but did not cut right through it, and it struck my horse's head, wounding it from its ears to the nostrils. Captain Skarzynski

9 Slang for Pole

accounted for two or three cossacks. Cossack lances are longer than ours, and in a close fight they handled less well. Our squadron repulsed this attack and sent the cossacks back to the shelter of their walls. Meanwhile, the Emperor had carried out his reconnaissance behind us and returned to his tent to issue instructions for the attack.

CAPTAIN SKARZYNSKI

The Polish infantry was able, with great gallantry under heavy fire, to reach the walls of the city, but could not get in as no breaches had been made. They lost many men, including General Chlopicki, who was wounded. The French infantry also launched several attacks on the left flank, but neither were they able to break in. I could not understand why the Emperor did not form a battery from the artillery reserve and blow holes in the walls before launching these attacks. They continued in vain until nightfall, when the Emperor did give orders for batteries to be deployed the next day. However, during the night we heard that our infantry had found a way into the city, which the Russians had evacuated. They had disappeared during the night across the Dnieper bridges.

It was a Polish brigade, consisting of the 15th and 17th infantry regiments, that had entered the city after finding a damaged section of wall that had only been plugged with bags of earth. They took with them two artillery pieces, commanded by Lieutenant Chrzanowski. In the order of the day, which the French called the bulletin, it was claimed that Frenchmen from Ney's Corps had been the first to scale the wall into the city. That was a lie, but the Emperor wanted to flatter his French troops.

Next morning, Davout's Corps marched straight through the town and across the bridges in pursuit of the Russians, who were now on the Moscow road. The Emperor occupied the city with the Guard and we stayed there for two days. On the evening of the second day the Emperor received reports that a horde of cossacks, followed by an entire Russian cavalry corps, had appeared from Mscislaw with the intention of attacking the part of our army that was still on the left bank of the Dnieper. Only the Polish Corps was over there, recovering from its heavy losses. The rest of the army, except for the Guard in Smolensk, had already crossed to the right bank. The Emperor summoned me and sent me with one squadron on a reconnaissance toward Mscislaw, to establish whether the reports of a Russian approach were genuine.

I led my squadron out of the city. While we were in Smolensk, we had been obliged to give the horses freshly cut rye. The men had had to sleep on the hard ground, as there was no straw. Half a mile outside the city I found Prince Poniatowski in his camp. He was sleeping in a shack, and I had to ask his a.d.c. to wake him, first to tell him I would be passing through his lines, and second to ask if he had received news of the enemy. He had been sleeping fully clothed,

THE POLES AT SMOLENSK

so came out to see me straight away and detailed an officer to lead me through his lines. The night was clear. We approached Prince Poniatowski's cavalry encampment, where we came upon Prince Sulkowski's cavalry division Sulkowski was also sleeping, but he too got up immediately; when I told him what my orders were, he said that a patrol had only recently returned from the Mscislaw road. Its officer had spoken to the local villagers, who could all speak Polish in this region, and who brought fodder and provisions to the camp. There had been no sign nor rumor of any Russians in the vicinity. Our horses were hungry, so I accepted an offer of forage. I decided I could rely on the report of this patrol commander, and after feeding our horses we returned to Smolensk at dawn. I only reported to the Emperor at 8 a.m., as I saw no need to wake him earlier to tell him the rumors had been false.

We left Smolensk about mid-day. A report arrived from Marshal Davout that he had encountered the Russians drawn up for battle about one and a half miles away along the Moscow road. His advance guard, which was Gudin's division, was already engaged. By the time we reached the field at about 4 P.M., the Russians had already retired. There were a lot of dead Russians around, and a disproportionate number of officers. General Gudin had lost both his legs and died. We heard that the Russians had fought very bravely among the pine

THE POLISH LANCERS IN ACTION

spinneys. The French called this the battle of Ten Leagues, for it took place that distance from Smolensk. Later they called it the battle of Valutin.

Three days after this engagement we reached Drohobuz. All the way from Smolensk the countryside had been arid and depressing, dotted with clumps, rather than forests of pines. It was very different from Lithuania, where the villages had been attractive and the agriculture well ordered. There, you could see the trace of the plough and human labor everywhere. Here, you found nothing except little village two miles or more apart. As the Russians retreated, they were burning most of the villages and forcing the inhabitants to load up their carts with their pitiful belongings and flee with their livestock to Moscow. Here and there peasants had made their way back. All the way to Moscow we found the odd local who could speak Belorussian or Polish. The same open countryside goes on as far as Viazma. The farmland around that town is much better, and there were some cultivated gardens such as might be found in the more rustic small towns of Poland. The Viazma market place and one or two streets even had brick houses, some of them with two stories. We found brick houses in Gracz as well.

On 5 September we finally arrived before a position that the Russians had strengthened with earthworks. Evidently they would accept battle here. That same day the 5th Corps, that is the Polish Army, stormed and took a large redoubt situated in front of the main enemy line. They performed marvelously but lost a lot of men.

The Emperor's tents were pitched inside this redoubt. The cavalry of the Guard made camp on the slope to the left and the Guard infantry and artillery encamped behind the Emperor's tents. Night was falling as the troopers drove their tethering rings into the ground. From Smolensk on, we had fed our horses exclusively on freshly reaped rye. In Lithuania and Belorussia, the peasants had been happy to sell us oats. But after Smolensk not only had the Russians taken everything and ejected the inhabitants, but the countryside was anyway very poor until only a few miles from Moscow. I don't understand how some authors can claim that Old Russia was a populous and prosperous country! It is quite untrue. The Russian peasant wears a long, coarse, dirty shirt, sewn together with straw or twine. Sometimes he wears a straw hat, and sometimes he is bare-headed. He wears his hair and beard long, and wears neither trousers or shoes. You can tell at first glance that his condition is miserable. I speak from first-hand, as we conducted numerous reconnaissances several miles to either flank and often came across local inhabitants, as the Russians were only evacuating people from a band about two miles wide in front of our advance.

Anyway, having pitched camp by the redoubt, Kozietulski and I lay down on our two saddle cloths and covered ourselves with our capes. It started to rain during the night, and as we were at the foot of the slope we were woken by a stream of water that had managed to find its way right between us. My left side was drenched, which is a horrible feeling when you want to rest. We had to get up and did not sleep again that night. Instead, we tried to warm ourselves by a cooking fire made by some of our troopers.

We stayed there throughout 6 September. The Emperor spent the day on horseback, riding along our picket lines, reconnoitering the enemy positions.

Before dawn on 7 September the bands on the right flank began playing the reveille to wake up the infantry, and it was gradually picked up all along the line. They played the most rousing pieces. Music does a great deal to prepare the spirit for battle. Nobody doubted anymore that there would be an engagement.

As soon as it was light, a short imperial proclamation was read out to each battalion. Soon after, the cannon opened fire on the left flank, heralding the attack launched by Prince Eugene Beauharnais.

This was the battle of the Moskova, as we named it after the river over which it was fought. The Russians, on the other hand, called it the battle of Borodino. I do not intend to describe it in detail, not least because it has been well chronicled by others: by Segur, who romanticized it a little too much; by Chambray, whose account was more military; and by Buturlin, who gave quite an honest account for someone who had been on the losing side. Anyway I could not follow events so clearly as I had been able to at earlier battles, when I had been with the Emperor who always placed himself at the best vantage points. On this occasion my regiment spent the whole time in a hollow, and all we could see was the smoke from the gunfire all along the line. Only once during the battle did we move to high ground, and that was for an hour

when our cuirassiers charged the enemy infantry in the central Russian redoubt. The Emperor ordered our regiment to move up in support and charge in turn if the cuirassiers were repulsed. This order reflected the Emperor's faith in us. The redoubt had been so ruined by cannon fire that the Emperor rightly judged cavalry capable of taking it. So we watched the beautiful sight of our cuirassier charge. It was made by four French regiments, by Poland's one and only cuirassier regiment under Malachowski, and by Leizer's Saxon regiment. The cuirassiers burst into the redoubt, sending the enemy

THE REDOUBT IS TAKEN

flying, and continued a good distance beyond. Malachowski and Leizer were both wounded several times and both unhorsed. After the redoubt was taken, my regiment retired to our original positions, protected from enemy fire. The only time any shots had come near to us was during that hour on the high ground when a few cannonballs had flown over our heads. We could see the Emperor pacing up and down constantly outside his tent, telescope in hand, but from this position he couldn't see the whole line, as our right wing [Davout and Poniatowski] were hidden by the wood on the old Moscow road. Moreover, Prince Eugene's left wing was hidden behind a hill line. All the Emperor could see was Ney's corps and the cavalry, which was almost entirely under Murat's command.

Every few moments a general would arrive from the front line and, so we were told, would beg the Emperor to release at least part of the Guard in order to decide the battle and exploit the victory. But the Emperor refused, and the only part of the Guard that was engaged that day was the artillery reserve of 60 pieces. Undoubtedly the Emperor wanted to keep the Guard intact because he was over 400 miles from France. Perhaps he also wanted to frighten Alexander into making peace by defeating him without having to use the Guard. It is certainly interesting that he specifically wrote in the following day's bulletin that the Guard had been inactive.

At about 4 P.M., an a.d.c. arrived to report that the Russians were in retreat. They were retiring in excellent order to Mozajsk and held that town for the rest of the night. Uncharacteristically, the Emperor did not order a pursuit. We could tell by looking at him that he was in some sort of pain that day. He alternated between pacing up and down and slumping in his chair. He did not mount his horse the entire day.

The day after the battle our regiment and the Dutch Lancers of the Guard (whose commander was Edward Colbert) set off to the south of the Moscow road with orders to cut the road between Moscow and Kaluga. After travelling about a mile from camp, we found the villages we passed through to be inhabited. In our regiment there were many soldiers and a good few officers from Podole, Wolyn, and the Ukraine. These could all speak Russian, or at least Belorussian. We always used to put one of these officers and a few of the men into our advance guard, and they would speak Russian to anybody we came across and pass themselves off as Muscovites. Some of the locals knew that their army had lancers from the Western provinces, so they easily mistook us for one of these regiments.[10] In the small towns we came across inhabitants who were better educated than the peasants. To begin with, as I said, they took us for Russian soldiers, but later, when they heard us speaking Polish and the Dutch speaking French, they guessed who we were. We made no attempt to claim otherwise, and found that they looked after us just as well and were even quite friendly toward us. A good many complained to us about their government. They would also warn us when cossacks were in the vicinity. All the same we placed outposts all around at night, normally with Poles in the direction of our march and Dutchmen in the rear. We also added one or two of our soldiers to each Dutch outpost to help with the language. One night, outside the large village of Faminskoi where we stayed for two nights, some cossacks ambushed and captured a whole Dutch detachment. Only one man, a Pole, escaped and raised the alarm. General Colbert mounted his horse and set off with two squadrons in pursuit, but the cossacks made off with

10 In fact, a Russian ulan regiment, recruited from Poles and dressed in blue like the Polish Guard Lancers, was in the area.

118

NAPOLEON BEFORE MOSCOW

their prisoners so quickly that all that could be seen were their hoof prints in the mud. The pursuit was called off after a mile or so, and they came back to camp. From then on General Colbert ordered that at least half of every detachment should be made up of Poles, and that sentries should thenceforward stand in pairs: one Pole and one Dutch lancer.

General Colbert spent every night in a tent, which used to be carried on a pack horse. It was so spacious that a dozen people could stand upright in it. He had two a.d.c.s, Bro and Bragues, both of whom could sing beautifully and knew all the pieces from the Paris vaudeville writers, Martine and Elseviou. Colbert would entertain a few of us in his tent every evening.

On our way from Faminskoi to Werca, we came across some new buildings, including a sugar refinery that had vast quantities of sugar loaf. All the troopers loaded themselves up with the stuff and ate it for several days. At that time the whole army had been suffering from dysentery because of bad food and bad water. Many men in our regiment had been affected, but after two days of this sugar cure, all traces of illness disappeared.

It was while we were there that one of our patrols captured a post chaise travelling on the main road from Kiev to Moscow. In it was Minister Guriew and his secretary. General Colbert sent them to the Emperor under escort.

At length we reached Podole, a town on the Moscow-Kaluga road. I left the regiment at that point, and went to Moscow to take over Imperial Household duty from Lieutenant

Colonel Jerzmanowski, who had been doing the job since we left Mozajsk. During our detached march to Kaluga we had spoken often to the locals and were convinced that nothing could be easier than to turn this oppressed people against its government. But the Emperor did not wish to contemplate such an act. During this march I concluded that the country people, the so-called serfs of Muscovy, were not as rich as Russians abroad like to assert. It's true they have a lot of livestock, but you can only see the mark of the plough in the immediate surroundings of the villages. Perhaps there are more prosperous regions elsewhere, but I had always heard that the richest lands were around Moscow, and I can't say I found any. It's true that in some villages close to the city we found well constructed and prettily painted houses for the peasants, but these were houses built at the expense of the rich landowners in the places where they had palaces. We did see some beautiful palaces and gardens along the road, tastefully constructed to a variety of styles, and well maintained. The peasant's houses near such places were solid and pretty, but often the very next village would consist of squalid huts with tiny farmyards, cattle byres close by, and no barns or outbuildings. There were no chimneys in these huts, and holes in the walls instead of windows from which the smoke would exit. They were so smokey that you could not stand in them, only sit or lie down. They had no bedclothes. Adults slept on benches, and children on the stove. We used to enter such dwellings, but obviously would camp outside the village at night.

We were seven miles from Moscow when the fire broke out. All night, despite this distance, we could see the fire reflected in the sky. The fire lasted several nights. The peasants watching the blaze with us declared that all Moscow must be aflame.

When we reached Moscow, I took over from the duty squadron. I was ordered to leave an officer and twenty five troopers in the Kremlin where the Emperor was, and take the rest of my men along Twerska street to the suburbs of Bialogrod and Kitajgrod. I was given quarters in the palace of Prince Lubanow. General Krasinski was across the street, in the palace of Barysznikow the banker. Both houses were very well appointed and in good condition. Upstairs and down, everything was very comfortable, and there were wide beds with padded mattresses. The facade of the palace looked onto the town, but behind it you could have been in the country. There were about a hundred Russians living in two houses in the grounds, a collection of servants, craftsmen, and peasants who we found ready to help us. There were tailors among them who we found particularly useful. They did all the work asked of them by the soldiers. These people served us peacefully and respectfully at all times. There was a good quantity of grain in store, which was most useful for the horses. It was said that three quarters of Moscow had been destroyed and only a quarter left standing, but I did not think so much damage had been done. The Kremlin, Bielograd, Kitajgrad, Twerska street, most of the suburbs on the west of the city, and nearly all of them on the Kaluga side were untouched.

Colonel Morawski visited us in our palace and stayed for a few days, as he was unwell. Young Caraman commanded a horse battery in Davout's Corps at that time and visited us often, despite being billeted nearly a mile away on the other side side of town. My batman at the time was trooper Marcin, who spoke good Russian and could procure anything for the right money.

By the time I had reached Moscow, the fires had all died out. The whole army was billeted in houses, and nobody was under canvas anywhere. I was told what had happened during the six days of the fire. Apparently there had been total disorder. All the officers agreed that if the Russians had attacked at that time, they would have won an easy victory. But now

THE LANCERS ESCORT NAPOLEON FROM MOSCOW

everything was under control again. In the undamaged houses and stores we found enough grain and victuals, so it was said, to feed the army all winter. To my disgust, numerous soldiers tried to sell to their comrades goods that they had looted for free. My troopers bought wine and food from such men. There were plenty of vegetables in the gardens in and around the city. There were vast stockpiles of fur coats and hats. Before leaving we equipped our entire regiment with fur hats. Detachments were sent for straw and hay to neighboring villages, having to go steadily farther afield. The cavalry of the Guard built up stores of fodder to see us through the winter.

The cavalry, under Murat, was based four miles from Moscow at Voronov. Poniatowski's V Corps was also there.

After a few weeks, the cossacks started attacking our forage parties. I was sent out often in search of them, but as soon as a few of our squadrons appeared, the cossacks would make themselves scarce.

The French officers found some French actors and arranged daily performances. The audience consisted exclusively of soldiers.

I went to several Russian churches. At one I heard the sermon, in which the pope preached against his government. I reckon he had been put up to do this by French officers, without the Emperor's knowledge, as he would have been very angry at attempts to stir up the serfs.

The army was in Moscow from 14 September to 20 October, when we began our march to Kaluga, but turned right at Malojaroslawiec and made our way back to Mozajsk. We had

COSSACKS ATTACK

only started the campaign in early June. If we had begun two months earlier, we could have retired to Lithuania while the weather was still fine. Even as it was, if we had spent only two weeks in Moscow and left on 1 October we would have reached the Dnieper in good weather. But the Emperor allowed himself to be fooled into thinking the Russians would make peace, as he so earnestly desired. An armistice had been agreed by Kutusov and Murat, when the Emperor sent General Lauriston to negotiate a peace settlement. But the armistice had been very fragile and could be broken by either side at only three hours notice.

While we spent five weeks in Moscow, Kutusov gathered all the reserves and recruits he could get from the depths of Russia. It was also said that the 12,000 Don cossacks who had completed their service had re-enlisted and that the Russian army had risen to 120,000 men. Our army, however, now amounted to barely 86,000.

On 18 October, the Emperor learned that a very angry Murat had renounced the armistice after cossacks had attacked our foraging parties, and that three hours later Kutusov had attacked him with such vigor that he had saved himself only with much difficulty, and with the help of Prince Poniatowski's V Corps. The Poles fought bravely on this occasion, as well.

On 19 October we were ordered to prepare to march, and on 20 October the whole army left Moscow except for the Young Guard that stayed behind with Marshal Mortier. He had orders to blow the Kremlin sky high, along with the arsenal in which 60,000 Russian muskets were stored. When the Russians had evacuated Moscow they had known we would have no use for these weapons but had not dared to distribute them among their militia, who were armed only with short pikes. They used the militia, which they called the "Druzyna," to guard stores and care for the wounded in battle. Four days later Marshal Mortier marched out, escorting a convoy of wounded, in the direction of Mozajsk. Instead of the main road, he went via Verija.

From Moscow to Malojaroslawiec our brigade was in the rearguard, but we saw no enemy at all for the first three days. Even when the Italian army began fighting at Malojaroslawiec, no cossacks appeared behind us. They did, however, emerge on our right flank to attack the Emperor's headquarters between Borowski and Malojaroslawiec. The only troops with the Emperor were our service squadron, under Lieutenant Colonel Kozietulski, who threw themselves at the swarm of cossacks. It was rumored that there were several thousand of them freshly arrived from the Don, and that Platov himself commanded them. Kozietulski was pierced by a lance, which entered his shoulder as far as the bone. For the remainder of the retreat he rode in a carriage, and later in a sledge, behind us. There then appeared the Horse Grenadiers of the Guard, in line formation. This line of black horses, its tall riders also in black bearskins, so impressed the cossacks that they disappeared into the forest. However, they reappeared half a mile further back to attack our brigade. General Colbert sent me with two squadrons to engage them. I advanced five hundred paces and stopped to rally a mass of French infantry who had been straggling behind their regiments and were now fleeing from the cossacks. There were about a hundred of them, who I placed in some huts on the left of my line. Our flankers did such a good job of drawing the cossacks onto the fire of this infantry that they were taken by surprise and retired, giving the rest of our brigade time to mount up.

General Colbert ordered my squadrons to return to the brigade and left a squadron of Dutch lancers under a captain in our place. The cossacks noticed the change immediately and attacked again, surrounding the Dutchmen on three sides. Seeing this, General Colbert ordered the whole brigade to charge. The cossacks retired to the tree line but were joined there by ten times their number. Our horses were tired out by their long charge and the cossacks pressed in on us from the front and sides. We lost twenty men and the Dutch lost over a hundred. This was the fault of General Colbert, who over-reacted to the threat to an isolated squadron by hurling everything he had at the enemy. We could have avoided suffering losses if he had charged with only a few squadrons and followed up with the rest of the brigade at a slow and orderly pace. You should never engage your whole strength at once, especially when dealing with cossacks. This was the worst loss we suffered during the entire Russian campaign. We would have lost far more men if the troops had not been experienced soldiers capable of defending themselves in single combat.

The Dutchmen were less experienced than our men and did not know how to handle cossacks. Every time they were in the rearguard they would lose a few men, and the cossacks were becoming increasingly bold in attacking them. One day General Colbert ordered a squadron of Poles to swap their white greatcoats for the blue Dutch ones. So dressed, they were to form the rearguard in the early morning before it grew light and see what happened. When the cossacks appeared they advanced boldly, preparing to charge. But as soon as our squadron advanced to meet them, they recognized our riding style and retreated, crying "Lachy! Lachy! [Poles! Poles!]."

At Malojaroslawiec the Emperor decided he had no option but to retreat in the face of Kutusov's doubled numbers. But instead of choosing the straightest and as yet unplundered route to Medym, Mscislaw, and Orszy, he took us through Borowsk, Wereje, and Mozajsk along the main road by which we had already come and which had already been stripped of resources. This decision is hard to explain, as the Medyn road was both untouched and shorter. For that reason Kutusov himself took it and reached Viazma after the Emperor and the Guard had passed through but ahead of the rearmost French corps. The Italians, Ney, and Davout had to fight their way through Viazma and lost many men in the process. But they caught up with us at Smolensk, where the Emperor stopped for two days and the Army set off in good order once more. Marshal Ney and the rearguard were a day's march behind the main body. We reached Krasne in two more days. While we were there, the Russians attacked the Young Guard from the direction of Smolensk, cutting us off again from the Italians, Davout, and Ney. The Emperor ordered his a.d.c., General Durosnel, to take a Guard battalion and my two squadrons and reopen the road for Davout. It was a clear night when we set off, and the cossacks retreated before us. A mile along the road we saw the fires of the Russian camp. General Durosnel considered it too strong for us to attack, so he ordered me to choose an able n.c.o. and two troopers to send around the enemy to the isolated corps and tell them the Emperor would remain in Krasne until they arrived. We returned at 3 A.M. to Krasne. At dawn the next day, the Emperor led the Guard back along the road toward Smolensk, but we halted before a deep snow filled gulley as we heard heavy cannon fire and musketry, coming steadily closer. The Emperor concluded that our rear corps were breaking through, and sure enough there soon appeared some small cavalry detachments, followed by Davout and his sadly depleted corps. At about mid-day the Italian Corps arrived, having lost all its artillery. The Emperor order the Polish Corps, which had not lost one cannon in the retreat, to give thirty pieces, half its total, to the Italians. If the truth be known, the Poles, who had lost a good many men at Woronow, were happy to relinquish them, and brought the remaining thirty safely back to Poland. This, in spite of their tough fight on the Berezina, which we will discuss below.

The Emperor waited one more day for Ney and returned to the same position behind the gulley, but instead of Ney we saw dense columns of Russians pouring out of Smolensk and moving to outflank us from the south. Some of their cavalry even appeared in our rear, and numerous light infantry appeared on the far side of the gulley. They even seized a village of about a dozen huts on our right flank and on our side of the gully. I was positioned to the right rear of the Emperor with four squadrons. King Murat dashed up and ordered me to follow him at the trot, which was not easy in the deep snow. We halted before the Russian occupied village, and he ordered me to charge right in ["entrez dedans"]. This was a peculiar order to give cavalry, but I had to obey. It was no wonder King Murat lost all the cavalry under his command during that campaign. Off I went into the center of the village. The Russian jagers fired at us from close range as we rode past the huts. I lost four men dead and six wounded, may they lie on Murat's conscience. The Russians didn't run away, nor could they in that impossible snow. It goes without saying that I had not dawdled in my pass through the village, but horses cannot gallop with snow up to their bellies. We came out the other side by the ditch and formed up again between the village and the Emperor, who was six hundred or so paces away. Then I saw a company of Guard Grenadiers approach the village, ordered up by the Emperor on seeing the mad order that Murat had given me. The Grenadiers took the village without a shot and the Russians retired to the far side of the ditch after barely one volley. Some of our men who had been unhorsed in the village were also freed.

The Emperor was on foot at the head of the Guard. I returned to my original position nearby. He was furious with Murat and shouted at me: "How could you obey the orders of that madman?" Howitzer shells began falling thick and fast among us and some of our men were hit. The Guard stood as solid as a wall. Our artillery behind the ditch didn't even reply, as the Emperor said the Russians were firing from too far away. Yet their shots still caught us from time to time. One shell landed next to the Emperor, who prodded it with his riding whip and said, "It's a long time since I've had these landing at my feet." The shell exploded and showered the Emperor with snow, but nobody was hurt.

As the Emperor saw more and more enemy troops approaching, he concluded that Marshal Ney had either been captured or taken a roundabout route to escape. We were therefore ordered to resume the retreat. We marched in a close column with the service squadrons in front, the Guard infantry in two columns with the artillery on the road between them, and the rest of the Guard cavalry right on the tracks of the infantry and guns. At

COSSACK

dusk we reached the little town of Lad, shadowed from the south by cossacks, and behind them regular troops. The cossacks kept up a constant fire on us with their light artillery. At times the shots landed close to the Emperor, who was walking on foot with the Grenadiers of the Guard. Our cavalry had to see the cossacks off with a number of charges.

The following day we marched in the same formation as far as Dabrowna. The cossacks caused us a scare during the night. Our sentries were posted all around, and very close to the huts on the edge of town. The people of Dabrowna are Poles, and they fed us generously. We were in dreadful shape by that time. From Dabrowna to Orsza we had a much quieter march and didn't see the enemy once.

The evening we reach Orsza I was ordered by the Emperor to take a squadron up the Vitebsk road. It was as if he had a premonition that Ney was coming from that direction. I duly set off. A few horsemen appeared, whom we took to be cossacks in the moonlight. When they saw us they ran away. Two miles further on we heard musket fire. At daybreak we came across a handful of cavalry followed by infantry, whom we recognized at length to be ours. Unable to break through along the main road, Marshal Ney had struck north, guided by a Belorussian peasant who could speak Polish. He had crossed the Dnieper, abandoning his artillery and many of his horses which couldn't cross on the thin ice, and followed the right bank of the river until he met us. He rode alone on an exhausted horse with only a few hundred men under arms and as many again who had thrown away their weapons from fatigue. He was overjoyed to

NAPOLEON DURING THE RETREAT

see us and to learn that the Emperor was waiting at Orsza only three hours away. His officers described their adventures during the gruelling few days. There were two or three Polish officers with the marshal, to whose linguistic skills he said he owed his salvation.

When we got back to Orsza, one of our troopers reported that, while on patrol on the far side of town, he had recognized my friend Caraman in a group of artillerymen gathered round a fire. He was in a dreadful state. All our troopers knew him, as he had often visited us in Moscow. As soon as I heard this news I went in search of him and found him in a very weak state. I could not stay with him long, as I had to return to Orsza, but on my return I sent an orderly back to him with one of my horses. They joined us just as we were preparing to leave the town, and Caraman stayed with me until we reached Poznan. He had commanded a horse

THE POLES AT THE BEREZINA

artillery battery in Davout's Corps, but he had lost it at Viazma. His horse had been killed and his orderly with his remounts captured, and he had marched on foot since Viazma.

At Orsza I also bumped into my old colleague Tascher, the Empress Josephine's cousin, who had lost his horse and was on foot. I gave him one of my horses, the one that a cossack lance had wounded at Smolensk. I had started with nine horses, and had seven left. They were all still in good condition, as every night an officer would take a party of troopers, riding little peasant horses kept for this purpose so as not to tire their own, on foraging expeditions to surrounding villages. They rarely came back empty-handed. One day they even returned with a Russian supply wagon, loaded with oats and provisions. They had come across a village occupied by Russian cavalry who had stabled their horses and bedded down for the night, not expecting any attack. The wagon's horses had been left in harness. So little did they fear us that they had placed no sentries at all, but simply huddled indoors to escape the cold.

From Orsza to Borysow we passed through great forests, along a road made of pine tree trunks that we could make out in spite of the snow. We were no longer suffering such hardship. The inhabitants were Latvians, who were most friendly toward us. The Emperor intended marching along the high road through Borysow to Minsk where there were large magazines, but on the day we left Orsza he received the bad news that General Dabrowski had been forced out of Bobrujsk by Cziczakow's army and was now retreating to Borysow. Dabrowski had bravely tried to keep the bridge across the Berezina open, but in the face of superior numbers he had been forced to burn and abandon it. The Emperor heard also that General Kossecki's newly formed Lithuanian brigade had been smashed and Minsk occupied by the Russians; that Schwarzenberg and Reynier were retreating to Warsaw under pressure from Tormansow; that General Konopka had foolishly accepted combat at Slonim and been captured with half of his regiment of Lithuanian Guard Lancers by Czaplic's Russian cavalry division; and that, to cap it all, Marshals Victor and Oudinot had been defeated by Wittgenstein's Corps and were retreating from Plock, and General Wrede was retiring before General Steindel's Finnish corps. It seemed that retreat across the Berezina was becoming impossible as the Russian plan was obviously to join up from the north and south and bar our way. And they would have achieved this if Kutusov, who was following closely behind us, had pursued us more closely, and if the Polish Corps, united with Dabrowski, had not managed by a Herculean feat to defeat Cziczakow.

Arriving at Borysow, the Emperor concluded that we could not cross the river there. He sent some engineer officers two miles up river and ordered them to build two bridges over the Berezina at Zemlin. Tomasz Lubienski's 8th regiment of lancers forded the river first and scattered Cziczakow's cossacks on the far bank. As soon as the first bridge was finished, Dabrowski's, Kniaziewicz's, and Zajaczek's divisions, the Vistula Legion, and Berk's cuirassier brigade all crossed and turned southwards to confront Cziczakow. The latter had been waiting for us opposite Borysow, but when he heard we were building bridges at Zemlin he set off to stop us. Half a mile from the bridges he was met and defeated by the Poles, and the rest of the army and the Guard were able to cross unhindered on the two temporary bridges. This, the last battle of the campaign, was fought and almost exclusively won by Poles, except for one brigade of French cuirassiers. General Dabrowski, Kniaziewicz, and Zajaczek were all wounded, Zajaczek having to have his leg amputated. Prince Poniatowski sprained his leg, so the Emperor gave command of the Poles to Marshal Ney.

The stragglers of the army, mostly wounded and such, were still streaming across the bridges when Marshal Victor reached them, with Wittgenstein in close pursuit. Russian cannon balls began landing among our wounded lying on the far side of the bridge. The Emperor marched off with the Guard along a narrow causeway through marshes that were not completely frozen over. We had to lay a dozen or so temporary bridges and arrived at length at Molodeczna. Behind us marched the Polish Corps that had beaten Cziczakow, and Victor's Corps brought up the rear. On the third day after crossing the Berezina, we reached Molodeczna without mishap. There the Emperor decided to hurry back to France to oversee the creation of a new army. But it was not until the following day, at Smorgona, when he handed over supreme command to Murat and set off in two carriages, one with the Emperor and Caulaincourt, and the other with Duroc and his a.d.c., Mouton. Wasowicz and Rustam, the mameluke, rode on sleds.

We arrived at Vilnius and stayed for two days. We then set off for Kovno. As we marched out of Vilnius we came across a scene of dreadful disorder and confusion, as the caissons and wagons were trying in vain to scale the steep slopes of the Ponarska hill. As I knew the area well, I led my cavalry off to the right, and by crossing the river Wilia on the ice, we avoided the traffic jam on the hill. Prince Carygnan's savoyard cavalry regiment followed us over.

At the start of the campaign our regiment had crossed the Niemen with 915 men. We provided cadres for the cavalry of the Lithuanian army and for the squadron of volunteers from Gdansk, and in addition three of our captains had been sent back with cadres from Moscow to form three new regiments that were never completed. Despite these detachments, we still recrossed the Niemen with 422 men, and were stronger than all the other three Guard cavalry regiments put together. I don't include the Dutch Lancers, because apart from Captain Colquhoun and his brother, who attached themselves to us, I saw neither sight nor sound of this regiment from Smolensk on. But you can't say we were spared from heavy duty. As soon as a report arrived from headquarters that there were cossacks about, the order would come down: "Polonais, allez vous. [Poles, off you go!]" It was a rare night indeed that we slept undisturbed.[11]

The chaos in the Army of the Rhine Confederation[12] was best illustrated by my encounter with the Bavarian commander-in-chief, General Wrede. It was the day after we reached Vilnius. The frost was twenty degrees below zero, one of the coldest days of the whole winter. In the morning I was on my way to Murat's headquarters in the citadel when I saw a man in civilian overcoat, wearing a bearskin hat and brandishing a sword, running down the street followed by twelve or fifteen soldiers with bayonets fixed, as if ready for a charge. When he saw me and recognized my uniform and czapka, he cried: "Where are the headquarters? There are cossacks in the city! They're snatching our men from the streets, but the Guard won't leave its quarters!" After staring at his face, partly hidden by a scarf, and hearing his voice, I recognized him to be General Wrede, whom I had seen frequently in 1809. I answered as calmly as I could: "I am just going to King Murat's headquarters now, and should be happy to take you there if you wish. But we need not panic, the gates are manned by our troops, and we have cavalry pickets all around outside the walls. There are no cossacks in the city yet, I assure you. I beg you to sheath your sword; we don't want to alarm King Murat."

Overall, the French officers bore the cold and the suffering far better than the allies right up to the end, and I am convinced that if the Emperor had only stayed with the army and pitched his tent at some base camp the generals would not have sloped away home, nor in turn the field officers and other ranks, and we could have kept the troops in order. The magazines which we encountered on our way back would have been emptied in an orderly way, instead of which they were plundered by one and all. But every time it came to a battle during the retreat, the French still won the day even when outnumbered.

Our regiment stayed in good shape to the last. The officers always slept by the camp fires among the soldiers. We did not really lack food, as we were close to headquarters and used to pay periodic visits to the cattle herd which had been brought along with the army. When

---

11 An interesting comparison with the figures in Scott Bowden's book, Napoleon's Grande Armee of 1813. Chlapowski has scant respect for the Dutch Lancers, and the reader will note that Chlapowski appears to discount them from his later accounts of 1813. In one respect, Chlapowski's figure of 422 deserves serious consideration; the Poles, whose homeland habitually suffered bitter winters, will have been better prepared for the hardship, mentally and perhaps physically, than their French and German allies. Combine their ability to cope in winter with the fact that the Guard had first pick of whatever was going, and 50 per cent losses appear less surprising. Remember also that the Polish lancers took part in no set piece cavalry battle.

12 The Rhine Confederation was composed of all Napoleon's puppet states in Germany.

we ended our march for the day, our lancers would take over some building or other and guard it to prevent the French from tearing it down for firewood. Our cook, Garolinski, and a dozen or so men would busy themselves inside cooking whatever they had collected. The soldiers would provide the meat and flour, and he would roast the meat and make patties with the flour which he would bake in the fire. We suffered badly for lack of salt.

Every morning before setting off, every trooper would receive a round of bread and a piece of meat, which were to last him the whole day. The lancers guarded Garolinski like hawks.

One day a few of us officers gathered in a hut to warm ourselves while we waited for our meat to cook. But as the hut heated up, it filled with an atrocious smell. Under a pile of straw we found the body of a Dutch general, who had frozen solid.

Before we reached Vilnius, a whole brigade of Neapolitans were frozen to death in one night. They cried to King Joachim for help, waving their frost-bitten hands, but nobody went to help them.

Once we had crossed the Niemen at Kowno, we no longer camped in the open, but always slept in villages. We spent a few days in Elblag, and at lengths reached Torun and finally Poznan. Here King Murat handed command over to Prince Eugene, who immediately began setting things in order and sent to the rear everyone and everything that was not fit for battle. It emerged that we had only 10,000 men fit for duty, most of them from the Old Guard, some companies of Italians, and sixty Bavarian light horse, who were put under my command, but impressed me only with their cowardice.

Viceroy Eugene heard that the Russian army had marched from Plock to Kalisz, and so he was obliged to quit Poznan. It was dreadful to have to leave the city, with the fear that I might not see my family home for a very long time to come. At 4 A.M. our last outposts retreated into the city before the enemy advance. Eugene had left with the main body the day before. Before dawn I sent most of the rearguard squadron after him and remained behind with a trumpeter and a few troopers in the market square, with twelve Bavarians on the far side of the bridge to discourage cossacks from crossing. When the Bavarians retired back across the bridge, chased by cossacks, and soon after I saw regular cavalry coming up Szeroka street, I decided with heavy heart to withdraw, and we filed slowly away past the town hall. The Russians, seeing our lance pennons, had stopped on the far side of the square. With my twelve Bavarians and six Poles I marched off after the squadron. It was eight in the morning on 12 February 1813.

We did not see the enemy again until Magdeburg, where our retreat from Moscow came to an end.

Marshal Bessieres, who commanded the Cavalry of the Guard, sent me to Frankfurt on Main to collect two thousand horses, which the German princes had offered the Emperor to remount the Guard. I was given an officer and a few old n.c.o.s from each regiment. This task took me a few weeks, during which, however, I was able to take some rest, as I stayed at the house of my colleague and friend, Tascher, who because of his poor health had been made governor of Frankfurt by the Emperor.

Prince Dominik Radziwill, who had commanded the 8th Lancers of the Duchy of Warsaw throughout the Russian campaign, was made second in command of our regiment, of which he was later to take full command at Leipzig. He was allocated billets in the town of Grimin, but shortly afterwards was sent via Frankfurt to Friedburg where he selected five hundred of the best men in Dabrowski's division for our regiment. We also absorbed the remnant of the

THE DEATH OF MARSHAL BESSSIÈRES

Lithuanian Guards, who had lost so many men at Slonim, including their commander General Konopka. In this way we doubled from five to ten squadrons, but six of these remained in Friedburg, and the other four, precisely those that had been to Moscow, went in April via Fulda and Weimar to the front line, commanded by Dominik Radziwill. I commanded the first two of these squadrons, and Jerzmanowski the second two.

The Emperor rejoined us at Nuremburg, The next day, 1 May, 1813, we were in a small engagement at Weissenfels. A line of enemy horse and artillery appeared on a far hillside. The Emperor sent Marshal Bessieres on a reconnaissance with the first of my squadrons. The Russians fired a few shots of cannon at us. A cannonball struck the marshal in the head, and the same ball also killed sergeant Jordan, the n.c.o. from my right hand squadron.

THE SAXON CAMPAIGN OF 1813

The Saxon Campaign began on 1 May 1813. The first shots were fired at the town of Weissenfels, and one of them, as I mentioned above, killed Marshal Bessieres, who was standing thirty meters ahead of my squadron, as well as my n.c.o., Sergeant Jordan.

The Emperor gave command of the Guard Cavalry to Marshal Soult. That same day we resumed our march with the Emperor. Enemy cavalry and artillery retreated before us until they reached Lutzen, where they had their headquarters. We made camp outside the town. On 2 May we continued on our way toward Leipzig. Prince Eugene's Corps marched in front, and behind him went the Guard. Marshal Ney's Corps marching on the right occupied the village of Kaja, and the rear was brought up by the corps of General Bertrand, the Emperor's aide de camp. All the corps advanced in tight columns, because we had only 200 cavalry with Prince Eugene, 1,600 with the Guard and 600 from the 10th Hussars with General Bertrand.

At about 10 A.M. we heard heavy cannon and small arms fire from the direction of Kaja. The whole Russian and Prussian armies had fallen unexpectedly upon Ney's Corps, which consisted entirely of young recruits ["premier ban"]. These had not been able to withstand the charges and heavy artillery barrage and fled Kaja. We arrived to find the whole corps fleeing in disorder, throwing its weapons away and scattering across the fields.

NAPOLEON RALLIES NEY'S CORPS AT LUTZEN

THE POLSIH LANCERS AT LUTZEN

It was a critical moment. The Emperor had been riding at the head of the Guard. He sent orders to Prince Eugene to turn and deploy at right angles to his line of march and advance to the sound of the guns. He then turned his own horse around, ordered the cavalry to follow him at the trot, and told the infantry (they were all Young Guardsmen) and artillery to follow on behind. Within half an hour we had arrived between a wood and the village of Kaja, and we deployed into a single line across the ground over which the last of Ney's recruits were fleeing. Within an hour the whole army of 120,000, which had been marching in columns to Leipzig where the Emperor had expected to find the enemy, had turned to face right in an easy maneuver. Only the Guard had been obliged to retrace its steps for half an hour in order to arrive at the crisis point facing the village of Kaja, which the enemy had occupied. When we arrived in front of the village, we were greeted with both artillery and small arms fire.

The Emperor ordered us to prevent the remnants of Ney's troops from passing through our ranks. The only way they could get past was around our left flank, in the gap between us and the approaching Young Guard. In this way, instead of scattering across the landscape, they gathered together, as they tried to escape from the enemy's fire. These were the last remnants, who had lasted longest in the village, and contained many officers and n.c.o.s. It was therefore easier to rally these old soldiers behind us, and moreover they had not discarded their weapons like the youngsters. But they were very few in number.

Our artillery arrived. The Emperor straight away ordered two batteries to unlimber on our left flank, and the Young Guard to form two columns behind us. The enemy had not advanced beyond the village but occupied all the houses, and a black column of cavalry formed up to the left of the village so close to us that we could make out a cuirassier regiment in its first line, next to a regiment of black hussars. We could even hear their officers shouting orders, in the lulls between the firing. We also saw considerable movement in the column behind these two regiments, and we were sure that they were preparing to attack and encircle our right flank. We prepared to receive them, but they spent too long getting ready and their best moment passed. In war, the commander must make decisions quickly. What is possible now might become unrealizable within five minutes. You have to be decisive and have a sharp eye for the opportunities.

More and more battalions arrived in our front line, and the Emperor ordered them to direct all their fire at the village. My two squadrons moved off to the right by platoons, whilst Jerzmanowski's moved to the left, and the Emperor drew his sword, placed himself between the two columns of Young Guard, and advanced through the resulting gap toward Kaja.[1]

THE YOUNG GUARD AT LUTZEN

The Young Guard stormed the village without firing a shot and ejected all the enemy with the bayonet. The enemy's fire from the surrounding gardens died away, and all this time their cavalry did not move. The tables had been turned, and in a moment our situation changed from defensive to offensive. Marmont's corps had appeared in the distance to our right, and perhaps this sight had checked the mass of the enemy cavalry. But I am sure an outflanking attack against the right of the French line would have stood a better chance of success if only

1 i.e. The two halves of the lancer regiment were drawn aside like curtains to allow the Young Guard to pass through.

they had tried it, instead of putting all their efforts into defending the villages of Rahna, Kaja, and Gorschen, which became their downfall.

Shortly afterwards, the Emperor sent for us and we advanced through the village, which was littered with dead and wounded. In some places, bodies were lying on top of one another. In one spot we saw a dead Prussian Grenadier, a giant of a man, and beside him, as if lying in his arms, a little French youth. General Lefebvre Desnouettes, who was riding at our head, looked at this pair and declared they could be father and son (this was the same General Lefebvre Desnouettes who had been captured by the English in Spain. I was told that having been placed in a small town somewhere in the depths of England, he had found a merchant who, for a hundred guineas, had arranged his escape to the coast, and he had been brought back to France one night by a smuggler).

On the far side of the village of Kaja we formed up behind the Young Guard, which was pursuing the retreating enemy.

On our left flank Prince Eugene had a tougher time against Wittgenstein's Russian corps, which only began to retire when the Prussian corps had retreated before the Young Guard and our artillery began firing into his flank. The whole enemy line was therefore in retreat, including the cavalry that had threatened our right. This was now retiring under pressure from Marmont's Marine corps, and Bertrand's corps further beyond. As I have said, we had no more than 2,400 horsemen in the army, so the Emperor did not wish to commit us. But we had been very lucky that the far more numerous enemy cavalry did not try anything.

At nightfall the Emperor ordered all corps to halt but to remain under arms. Before it became completely dark, we could see that the enemy cavalry had halted whilst their infantry continued to retreat.

Once night fell, the cannon stopped firing. General Lefebvre Desnouettes came to me and ordered me to follow him with one of our squadrons. Our infantry was about 1,000 paces from the enemy. We went out in front of them, and the General and I rode out a little further still. From there we could make out what seemed to be a line of soldiers against the horizon to our right. The General ordered the squadron to halt and sent me off with Lieutenant Leski to take a closer look. When we had moved 200 or 250 paces closer, we could not only see the line more clearly, but could also hear the jingling of harnesses. We turned and returned slowly toward the squadron, but as we moved off to the left we found a lone cavalryman, standing by his horse. As I came closer to him, I recognized a Prussian helmet, or it could have been Russian as they were identical. I seized his bridle, and he, apparently rather drunk, cried in German, "Wer da?" Having discovered his nationality I ordered him to mount his horse. Leski rode on one side, and I the other, and we took our prisoner back to our lines. He was not at all afraid, but only wanted to explain why he had left the ranks and dismounted. I told him to shut up, and despite being drunk he seemed to understand that he had to keep quiet. When we reached General Lefebvre, who was standing with his aide ten or fifteen paces in front of the squadron, I asked the cuirassier what was his regiment. He replied, "the First Brandenburg Cuirassiers."[2]

"Where is your regiment?"

"About 100 paces away, as I have only just left it."

2 The Brandenburg Cuirassier regiment was in fact numbered 4 in the Prussian army. However, regiments were also listed by seniority in each province, and this was shown by the color of their shoulder straps. The Brandenburg Cuirassiers wore the white straps of the first regiment in the province, although in truth they were also Brandenburg's only cuirassier regiment!

When I told the General what the prisoner had said, he drew his sword and cried aloud, "Ha! Ha! So they want to take us by surprise! We must charge them first! They won't stand a chance in the dark!"

By then the Emperor, who had come up behind our squadron without our knowing, joined us and said to him: "Lefebvre! You're always the same: still mad! [toujours fou]. The squadron will remain in place." Then he told me to question the Prussian cuirassier further. Either the man had finally realized we were the enemy and lost his nerve, or the drink was taking effect, but he said very quickly that twenty regiments were to attack the French camp at midnight (that must have been what their soldiers were told). The Emperor ordered us to retire, and we passed through the front line of infantry, who were still under arms. Soon the order circulated that one battalion from each division should advance hundred paces towards the enemy, form square, and await the morning.

MURAT

Sometime before midnight we heard the jangling of enemy cavalry to our front. Within ten minutes one of the squares at the right end of our line opened fire. We also heard a great deal of activity to our immediate front, but the square covering our part of the line did not fire at all. Our horses were so frightened by the firing of the square to our right that we had to reorder our line. Cavalry attacks can never work in the hours of darkness, as the smallest infantry line will stop them and force them to retire in confusion. That's exactly what happened with this Russo-Prussian attack. Undertakings like this should only be attempted in the hour before dawn, so that the enemy's confusion can be exploited if the surprise succeeds.

On this occasion, the Emperor lacked sufficient cavalry to place pickets or send patrols to cover the line, so was obliged to keep the front line of infantry alert all night. Perhaps he had also been tipped off about the enemy's intentions by a spy.

At 2 A.M. the Emperor stood down the first line, as the second line and reserve had had several hours' good rest. The second line then stood to arms from 2 A.M. to dawn.

Also, at 2 A.M., we rode back with the Emperor to Lutzen, and made camp outside the town, in the same spot where we had spent the previous night.

We did not get much of a rest, as at daybreak the Emperor left Lutzen and we with him. We passed through Kaja and caught up with the infantry, which was already en route to Pegau along the shortest major road to Dresden. This was a shorter march than our original destination of Leipzig.

Every day during our march on Dresden there were skirmishes between our advance guard and the enemy rearguard. On a few occasions my regiment was able to watch these encounters from high ground. They were unusual, because our side consisted only of infantry,

NAPOLEON AT THE CROSSING OF THE ELBE

and the enemy of numerous cavalry. The French infantry would advance in columns with voltigeurs out in front, but never too far out because this would be dangerous when facing cavalry, especially clouds of cossacks. The infantry would advance steadily until they encountered enemy artillery in any number, when they would deploy but continue to advance at the same pace. Artillery pieces would advance between the battalions, and would unlimber and fire whenever the enemy seemed ready to pass onto the attack. Undoubtedly, it is far preferable to have cavalry in the advance guard as well, but this march from Lutzen to Dresden, and then from Dresden to Bautzen shows that you do not need as much cavalry as is usually deployed, and frankly misused. Because advance guards have constantly to be on the their guard, horses have to be kept fully harnessed and ready for action, which tires them dreadfully as the retreat from Moscow had demonstrated. King Murat had always had masses of cavalry in the advance guard, yet often he would have to wait with all these horsemen for several hours, waiting for an infantry battalion to come up and clear a few hundred Russian jagers out of a wood! During these marches from Lutzen as far as Bautzen our infantry, never once came off badly, despite the absence of cavalry. They lost men from artillery fire, but not once did a cavalry charge against them succeed. I ought to mention however, while on this subject, the incident at Haynau after the battle of Bautzen, when an infantry advance guard was very badly handled. Maison's division halted for the day in front of this town instead of behind it, and after placing sentries very close to the main body, the men piled arms and went back to the town in search of provisions. Some enemy cavalry, which had been hidden in a wood nearby, fell upon the camp, sabring the sentries and caused havoc. They got right into the middle of the camp and disappeared within minutes. Not many men were lost, but this attack had a serious effect on our morale. None of this need have happened, if the division had halted short of the town, and sent one battalion to occupy the outskirts on the far side and place sentries a little further out in front. If an advance guard is unable to shelter in this way behind a town or village, but instead has to halt in the open, they must stay alert continuously, and only send out small parties for food, firewood, and straw. But the Grand Army was always careless in this respect. I repeat, it is not a good idea to have no cavalry at all in the advance guard, but in this campaign there was no alternative. It is much better to have just enough cavalry to do sentry duty, and above all to send out patrols and conduct reconnaissances. You don't need that many cavalry to perform this task. I am personally convinced that the bulk of the cavalry should be kept in reserve, for use in battle and during the pursuit. I am not trying to spare the cavalry. On the contrary, I believe it should be used with the utmost boldness, but at the right time and place. I don't want it to stand deep in reserve during the battle; let it stay close behind the infantry, or even beside it if the terrain is open, and be ready to smash the enemy the moment the opportunity to attack arrives. It's true that you lose more men from gunfire in the front line than if you stand far in the rear, but experience shows that cavalry which has withstood bombardment for a few hours attacks all the more vigorously when its time comes, however many men it has lost. I don't want to save cavalry from bullets, only from pointless dashing about. The French never could use cavalry sparingly. Except during the Saxon campaign, they always placed far too many in the advance guard and used more men than were necessary in patrols and reconnaissance. The result was to exhaust the horses and lose a lot of men, especially against cossacks, who were always setting ambushes and were very clever in that kind of warfare.

We entered Dresden Old Town unopposed on 8 May. The bridge across the Elbe was half destroyed, and the Russians were in the New Town with cannon along the river that fired at anyone who approached the bank. The Emperor ordered his aide de camp, Caraman, to take a battery of Guard artillery to the river bank. It was a tonic to see how this officer instilled calm and confidence into both officers and gunners. This battery of six guns had fired no more than three or four volleys before it created great disorder on the far bank. Within half an hour the Russian guns had disappeared and the rest of their army with them.

The French engineers were posted to the left of Dresden. There they threw a bridge across the river, under the cover of a sixty gun battery which General Brouot had placed on the heights of Prusnitz. That same day planks were laid across the destroyed span of the main bridge. On the 10th the Viceroy of Italy's corps crossed the river and marched on Bautzen, with Marshal Marmont hurrying close behind. The Emperor left with the Guard a few days later, on the 18th, having waited for the return of the King of Saxony, who had taken shelter from the Russians in Prague.

We covered the march from Dresden to Bautzen in one day. That same evening, 18 May, the Emperor spent almost the whole night riding along our picket line, studying the enemy positions by the fire of their bivouacs. The Emperor expected them to defend the strong position around Bautzen, which lent itself to fortification. To the left were some quite pronounced ridges, while to the right began the chain of hills that separate the Czech lands from Saxony. The Emperor decided his dispositions for the following day and all the corps moved forward in a line: Oudinot on the right, Marmont in the center opposite Bautzen itself, and Marshal Ney, who was ordered to march from Hoyerswerda to form our left flank.

We set off with the Guard in the center, but saw no enemy infantry or artillery, only detachments of ulans and hordes of cossacks retreating before us.

We passed Bautzen and marched off to the left. We crossed the river Spree, which was nearly dry, and only after we had marched a further half mile beyond Bautzen did we encounter the enemy line, around Hochkirch.

Evening was already approaching. At sunset the Emperor returned to Bautzen, where quarters had been prepared for him in the bishop's palace. As soon as we reached the city, we were given our billeting dockets. We stabled our horses peacefully, removing their harnesses (except for the service squadron) as if it were peacetime. The inhabitants were still in their houses, and we found suppers prepared for us. This was the most delightful night we ever spent so close to the enemy. But the infantry was protecting us in its positions outside the town, and every effort was being made to spare what little cavalry was left after the Russian campaign.

Before dispersing for the night, we had been instructed to harness our horses by 4 A.M. ready to march. In the end, we only moved off at 7 A.M. with the Emperor, and the whole cavalry of the Guard, that is four regiments, drew up in a single line on a prominent position well within sight of the enemy in Hochkirch. We formed the center of the line and maintained communications between the left and the right wings. Marmont's corps and Latour-Maubourg's cavalry had been shifted from the center to the left wing, because Ney had sent word from Hoyerswerda that he was marching along a very difficult road and would only reach the battle line at mid-day. When the Emperor received this news he delayed the planned infantry attack, but the cannon kept up a constant bombardment and a lively skirmish broke out among the bushes on the hills on our right flank.

The Emperor lay down on his spread overcoat, and after instructing that he be woken in two hours, he fell asleep to the tune of this violent music.

For the next two hours, the skirmishing continued on the hillside to our right, punctuated by the fire of a dozen or so cannon that the French had manhandled up the slopes. The enemy had more guns than us in place, as he had had ample time to prepare his position. In the center we were faced by cannon fire alone, and only very limited skirmishing in the valley to our front. From time to time cannonballs would reach as far as our position, fired by the enemy's heavy artillery. But the dozen or more bouncing shots that reached us were losing force, and none caused us injury. One howitzer shell exploded near the Emperor.

At about 1 P.M. the 7th Lancer regiment[3] arrived, and what a beautiful sight it was. It was the old Polish regiment that had been through all the Italian campaigns, and now had been transferred from Spain and brought up to strength in Sedan with reinforcements from the Polish corps on the Rhine. Its commander was Stokowski, our former lieutenant colonel who now had the rank of general.

---

3 Better known as the Vistula lancers. Chlapowski describes their arrival at Bayonne in 1808 (see above). This was the regiment he asked to join in 1810 because they, unlike the Guard, were on active service at the time.

FRENCH COLUMNS ATTACKING

Stokoski had remained in Sedan to form two more squadrons, and meanwhile Colonel Tanski was in command. The regiment drew up to our left and extended the line of the Guard cavalry.

The Emperor was still sleeping when the Imperial aide de camp, Berenger, arrived from Marshal Ney with the news that after picking its way along the sandy tracks, his corps was now deploying opposite the right wing of the enemy position, which was on a hill that had been well fortified with earthworks. Marshal Duroc, who was standing by the sleeping Emperor, did not see the need to wake him until the two hours were up. Such was the habit now instilled in his staff to obey the Emperor's orders to the letter! Duroc simply took out his watch, and said, "Another twenty minutes."

The twenty minutes had not yet passed when we heard an eruption of cannon fire from the Russian positions to our left. We could see the smoke, and also the flashes from the muzzles. The fire was so sudden and intense that it woke the Emperor, who cried, "Ney must attack!" He mounted his horse and sent off his aides with orders to all his marshals to attack, adding as he did so: "Victory will be ours within the hour!" But he misjudged the time it would take, for an hour later the enemy's right wing was still in place, and its artillery fire, now supported by musketry, was, if anything, livelier than before. Every ten minutes or so the Emperor sent off another officer to find out what was happening, but none of them returned. The Emperor was on horseback about fifty paces in front of us. I had moved forward from the main body to gain a better view of events. The Emperor turned, and failing to locate any aide de camp nearby he called to me: "Klaposki," (for that's how he, and indeed all the Frenchmen, pronounced my name), "go to Ney and tell him to hurry up and attack with everything he has got. Marmont has now reached him and will support his attack."

I found the Marshal in the thick of the firing, among his infantry columns that had been repulsed and were reforming to try again. The first troops I encountered were Wurtemburgers, who were retreating in the utmost disorder, then Frenchmen who were in better shape, but also in retreat. I repeated the Emperor's message. Ney bowed and replied: "Go back straight away, and tell the Emperor that I am facing Russians. If they had been Prussians, I'd have taken the position long ago. I'm going to try again with our boys [i.e. French troops]. I've sent the allied troops to the rear; they're no match for the Russians."[4]

Some four French columns had come up from reserve and were marching past the troops that had been repulsed. Marshal Ney rode up to each one and urged it forward with some rousing words and a wave of his hat. The grenadier companies at the head of each column fixed bayonets and set off at the fastest possible pace up the hill. A lot of them fell, but it didn't last long. They had got within two hundred paces of the summit and the Russian batteries when the firing stopped. When they reached the rest, they found the entrenchments empty of enemy. We hurried up between the middle two columns and reached the hill top, from which a beautiful sight presented itself. The Russian infantry were in full retreat, and the tail ends of their columns were already disappearing behind Weissenberg,. They must have abandoned their positions at least half an hour before. The artillery was following behind at a trot, and on the plain between us and Weissenberg stood two lines of enemy cavalry, about 6,000 horsemen, covering the retreat of the artillery.

The Russians had thus retired just in time to avoid further losses. Their commander,. Wittgenstein, must have concluded, either that the French could carry the position this time, or that Marmont's corps which was approaching the village of Boschwitz was about to attack his left flank.

There are two Acts in an attack on an entrenched position. In the first, the attacker loses a great many men from fire, to which he is unable to reply. In the second, the defender will lose far more men if he stays put, because when the attacker finally storms the position, nothing can stand in the way of his bayonets. The Russians on this occasion played the first Act to perfection, and very wisely avoided the second. They retired just in time, in the best possible order, and with cavalry support which we had no way of challenging.

I returned to the regiment, which I found marching after the Emperor toward Hochkirch. I saw no need to give him a report, as I knew he would have had a clear view of what Marshal Ney had done.

It was already growing dark when we marched into Hochkirch, so we could not see the entrenchments which the enemy had dug in front of the village. He had abandoned them as soon as the right wing had retired. We made camp to the left of Hochkirch at a village in which the Emperor's quarters had been prepared.

---

4 It is interesting that here, as at Lutzen, the clear message is that, in French eyes, Russians were a tougher nut than Prussians. The answer does not lie in the Prussian use of landwehr (militia), for these formations were not yet in the field. Perhaps the Prussians were still shaking down, having had little experience on active service since 1807. Or maybe the French were still conditioned by their memories of Prussian performance in 1806-7, and instinctively dismissive. Finally, it just may be true that Russians dug in behind field fortifications were a tougher enemy than their allies.

On the following day, 22 May, we set off with the Emperor to Zgorzelce [Gorlitz]. After two hour's march, we heard cannon and small arms fire in the distance to our front. Soon, Marshal Soult, who had replaced Bessieres in command of the Guard, came up and ordered General Walthier, the commander of the cavalry, to take all his regiments off to the right, until we came abreast of a hilltop from which the Russian rearguard was blocking the army's advance through Reichenbach. Having drawn level with this hill, we were to turn left and force the enemy to abandon his position by attacking him in his left rear. We marched off by platoons, and crossing the fields at a trot we covered about half a mile until we came to a deep ditch, full of trees. There we had to halt and cross slowly in pairs. As soon as my two squadrons had crossed, General Lefebvre Desnouettes, who had been marching at our head, ordered me to see off a mass of cossacks

JANKOWSKI

that had appeared to our front. I formed line with my two squadrons and advanced toward the enemy. The cossacks retired before us firing their side arms. We followed them for three hundred paces, while the next two squadrons under Jerzmanowski crossed the ditch behind us. We came upon a second ditch, only shallower this time. The cossacks halted on the far side, and kept up a lively fire from behind the trees. They began moving toward us again, but as soon as we had begun to cross this ditch in a couple of places, they resumed their retreat. When we had crossed the second ditch, we saw a line of regular cavalry beyond the cossacks. After we had advanced five hundred paces I could make out four squadrons: two of dragoons in the center, with one of lancers on either side.

Once my squadrons had crossed the ditch and reformed into line, we began slowly to advance. General Lefebvre arrived in a rush and said I should charge. But he did not say this as an order, and he added that he trusted my judgement. Had he given me a clear order I would, of course, have ordered, "trot," and then, "gallop." Incidentally, there's no need to order the troops to charge after they have begun the gallop: experience shows that nobody can be expected to issue orders as if on parade.

We were still about five hundred paces from the enemy, so I said to the general, who was riding beside me: "If you permit me to advance at a walk for another 150 paces, and then to move straight into a charge, I vow I can shatter the enemy's center." He agreed and returned to the squadrons that were crossing the ditch behind us.

We continued at a walk for another three hundred paces, and I instructed both squadrons to go hell for leather as soon as I sounded the charge. They were not to lower their lances, however, but should point them at the enemy's faces. We got so close to the enemy line that we could hear the voices of their officers, reassuring the soldiers with the word: "Szutka!" [It's a ruse]. We were perhaps two hundred paces away when I ordered, "Charge!" and in the blinking of an eye we were upon them. Captain Jankowski was on my right and Lieutenant

JERZMANOWKI

Gielgud was on my left. The latter's horse had just forced its way among the dragoons when one of their officers stabbed him in his stomach and he was unhorsed (he died several weeks later).

The melee lasted but a few seconds. From the moment we struck, the enemy fell into confusion and began to retreat, even including the ulans who had no foe to their front. I did not see how many men fell because I had passed through their line so quickly. My squadrons had themselves become disordered and individuals were chasing after those of the enemy whose horses were weakest, and ordering them to dismount. But shortly I saw a second enemy line approaching, all of them ulans. I stopped my horse, and had only begun to restore order to the ranks when this line began a charge. I was obliged to reform as best I could and order, "Forward! March!" otherwise they would have caught us stationary, which you should never let the enemy do. Indeed, we had just charged and beaten twice our number of dragoons and ulans because they had received our charge at the halt. We had not even noticed the point blank carbine fire of the first enemy line, as this kind of pot-shotting has no effect on veteran troopers. So anyway, in response to the charge of the second line I ordered, "March!" and then, very quickly, "Charge!"

As they charged, the Russian ulans lost some of their dressing, but they still came on and broke into our line. They outnumbered us, and we should certainly have been beaten if Jerzmanowski had not come up with our second pair of squadrons. He was the very best field officer in the regiment, by far the most experienced and with a fine, cool judgement. At just the right moment he struck the enemy from our left flank, having come up close at a walk to save energy for his charge. The ulans retreated almost faster than they had charged. A dozen or so fell into our hands. One or two of their wounded were crying out in Polish. This upset me greatly. One of them was still brandishing his sword and refusing to surrender, until one of our troopers said, "Comrade, we're Poles like you." At that he dropped his sword instantly. He must have been told that although dressed like Poles, we were in fact Frenchmen.[5]

5 The Russians, like the French and Austrians, regarded Poles as natural horsemen, and the lancers as a Polish weapon. They therefore recruited heavily in Polish-speaking areas to fill their ulan regiments. There was even one Russian formation entitled the Polish ulan regiment. The uniform worn by lancers throughout Europe well into the 20th century was modelled on Polish dress.

CHLAPOWSKI AT REICHENBACH

At the very moment the enemy had charged us, an old bearded cossack had appeared from nowhere beside me. He was on foot, and grabbed the left side of my horse's bridle as he aimed his pistol at me. Meanwhile an ulan officer had arrived and was going for me with his sabre. I parried this attack, and just as the cossack was ready to fire, he fell, run through by the lance of chevauleger Jaworski, who received the cross [of the Legion of Honor] for saving my life. Years later I met him again in Maluszyn.

The ulans had disappeared, and our four squadrons reformed into line. We had advanced quite a way ahead of the Chasseurs à Cheval of the Guard, who were crossing the ditch behind us, and so General Lefebvre ordered us to halt. Then another regiment of Russian ulans appeared from the direction the other had vanished, and advanced toward us in line. But when it was still five hundred paces away it broke into a gallop. General Lefebvre, who was standing with Jerzmanowski and me, again wanted us to counter-charge. Jerzmanowski, who knew Lefebvre very well, told him there was no point in charging, as the enemy had begun to gallop far too soon; they would soon lose formation and would never reach us. Sure enough, their line shortly broke up, a few dozen pulled ahead and the majority began to slow down. Nobody came any closer to us than a hundred paces.

Lefebvre ordered two platoons to form skirmish order and go out to meet them. They brought back half a dozen or more of the slowest horsemen. We discovered they weren't lancers, but regular Ukrainian cossacks. One of them, a Belorussian, told us in quite good Polish that there were four regiments of them under General Witt, but that he was not present on the field.

The cossacks had retreated and were reforming a very long way away from us. This proved them to be very young recruits, whose officers were probably no better. I should add that their hearts were not in the fighting because, as I later discovered, these were men who had been raised by the Ukrainians the previous year to serve the French. When we had been kicked out of Russia, four regiments of these recruits had been offered to the Emperor Alexander to disguise these preparations.

Anyway, the Ukrainians had fallen back before us and from then on all we saw were Don cossacks in the far distance. Now General Walthier appeared, and after complimenting us on our charge he ordered us to march off by platoons to the left and advance up the slope toward the position from which the enemy rearguard was blocking our infantry's passage through Reichenbach. Their commander was General Miloradowicz. He had about forty cannon which were positioned to fire right down the main street of the town and forced the French infantry to take shelter behind the houses.

Jerzmanowski, who was on my left, reached the hilltop first and formed line, and my two squadrons formed up to his right. As soon as Jerzmanowski appeared, the Russians turned some of their cannon to fire at him and at my squadrons as they deployed. At the same time a regiment of enemy hussars appeared a few hundred paces from our right flank; so I was obliged to turn to face them with my two squadrons. But in the process of turning, we presented our flank to the enemy cannon, so that they caught us in enfilade. Thus, in the space of ten minutes, we lost more men than in all of the charges we undertook that day.

Jerzmanowski's squadrons, being closer to the enemy cannon than we, lost even more men as they also turned to face the hussars. But as soon as our line was in order we began to charge. When we were about sixty paces from the hussars they turned and fled, and did not stop until they had passed through a regiment of cuirassiers, behind which they began to reform. Our earlier position facing the enemy artillery was occupied by the Chasseurs à Cheval of the Guard. The Dragoons and Horse Grenadiers of the Guard stood in lines behind the crest of the hill, and, as I later discovered, they lost more men there from the enemy fire than we had done on the forward slope. This was because the Russians were firing bouncing shot, and the cannon balls and shells were striking the earth in front of us, bouncing over our heads, and frequently landing on the far side of the hill. Before our charge, our four squadrons had stood in line for a certain time, a little in front and downhill of the crest, with a valley between us and the Russians. At one point I had just moved over to talk to Jerzmanowski, when first one, then a second and a third ball landed just where I had been standing and bounced over the heads of the squadron. The Chasseurs à Cheval who took our place on the forward slope also lost fewer men than the Dragoons and Grenadiers.

Shortly after we had charged the hussars, the Chasseurs à Cheval came over to support us. General Walthier must have seen the line of enemy cuirassiers. First came the mamelukes, who made up the first squadron of the Guard Chasseurs; they came up on our left and launched a charge straight into the cuirassiers. The enemy commander could not have believed that a single squadron would attack his brigade, which was drawn up not in one, but in two lines. The Mamelukes advanced at the walk, and at fifty paces or less they fired their blunderbusses. The right wing of the cuirassiers promptly turned tail and ran, taking the rest of their line with them! It's true that our four squadrons were also advancing toward the cuirassiers, but they gave us no chance to attack as they retreated in a rabble upon their second line.

We were promptly ordered back to our original position, facing Miloradowicz's guns. This had been occupied by a regiment of Saxon cuirassiers in yellow jackets, which I had never

THE PRUSSIAN CAVALRY MAKE THEIR SURPRISE ATTACK

seen before. But it must have been a newly formed unit made up of recruits, as its officers could not keep them in this exposed position and so we had to take their place again.

Now Miloradowicz's guns redoubled their fire to cover his retreat. As soon as we had replaced the Saxons, a hail of balls and shells came in our direction, but very few actually hit our ranks. One shell exploded between me and Captain Jankowski. A fragment struck his lip, but only lightly, and another hit me with more force on the right shoulder. But I was able to stay on my horse, and only dismounted when the fighting was over.

Some way behind, between our position and the French and Saxon infantry which were now advancing through Reichenbach, stood General Latour-Maubourg's cavalry. They lost a few men from cannonfire, but did not otherwise engage the enemy.

Miloradowicz began his retreat, and his guns moved off among his infantry columns. Behind him French infantry came fanning out of Reichenbach, and French skirmishers appeared on the hills to either side. Soon the Russian infantry disappeared from view, and only a few light guns and cavalry remained to exchange fire with us. Then the Emperor set off for Zgorzelice, with us behind him. One of the last shots of the day landed near the Emperor and mortally wounded Marshal Duroc, who died that night. The Emperor had intended to take Zgorzelice that same day, but when Duroc was hit, he ordered his tents to be erected on the spot and spent nearly the whole night by the dying marshal.

We spent the night with the rest of the cavalry by a wood near the Emperor's tents. As I prepared to dismount and shifted my weight onto my right arm, I felt a sharp pang of pain.

The following day I could not shave as my right arm was bandaged, and for the first time in my life I had to use my left hand.

But I as very flattered that evening in camp, when Generals Walthier, Lefebvre, and LeFort all congratulated me on my successful charges. I was delighted when one of them said: "If anyone is braver or fights better than us, it's you Poles!" You have to have a very high opinion of your own valor to say something like that.

This combat at Reichenbach took place on 22 May. It is memorable, in that the French cavalry, despite its small numbers, won the day almost single-handed.

The next day we passed through Zgorzelice on the road to Boleslaw, and camped for the night at Waaldau. On the 25th we moved beyond Boleslaw, and on the 26th we passed Haynau. That was the day the Prussian cavalry attacked Maison's infantry division, which had unwisely camped in front of the village, stacked its weapons, and gone looking for food and straw in the village. Only a few soldiers, perhaps two hundred, had remained on guard.

The Prussian cavalry made their surprise attack, emerging from a small wood on the left of the road. They must have seen from that position that the French had piled arms and gone off toward the town. So they charged, overturned the pickets, scattered the abandoned weapons, and disappeared.

This surprise attack would not have happened if General Maison had made camp behind the village and placed one battalion in the building on its far side. Nor, lacking any cavalry, should he have placed his pickets so far away from the village.

We arrived at Haynau a few hours after this incident and there was no longer any sign of the attack, except for 150 men dead and wounded. Very few muskets had been broken, and no cannon had been carried off because the drivers had led the teams away in search of fodder. We camped at Haynau that night, and on 28 May the Emperor arrived. He formed all the infantry into two columns of battalions, that is, each with the frontage of one battalion. The cavalry and artillery rode with the Emperor between the columns, and we marched thus from Haynau to Lignica, a distance of two miles on an open plain. It was very fine to see these 100,000 men in two great columns marching across an area so flat, that we could see along their entire length at the same time. We arrived before Lignica, and the Emperor ordered Marshal Soult to take the Guard Cavalry and circle the town from the right, in order to catch any enemy that might still be retreating from the far side.

We set off at a trot. We had to pass through a long village straggling along to the south of Lignica, through the middle of which ran a little stream with a narrow bridge which slowed us up considerably, As soon as my two squadrons had crossed, I led them rapidly out of the village, leaving the rest of the column behind, for I had seen some individual horsemen retreating before us. When we arrived in the open again I saw four squadrons standing in line. So I turned my line to face them and just as we did so, they began to advance and their trumpeters sounded the charge. I advanced to meet them. Their officer must have been inexperienced, for as soon as he had ordered the charge, his trumpets sounded, "Halt!" They stopped, turned right around, and began to retreat just as we fell upon them. As might be expected, they routed. Their slowest troopers fell into our hands and we'd have captured more if their infantry had not been in column close by. It was marching faster than any Prussian infantry I had ever seen, retiring from Lignica to Jaworz. We could have captured their whole division (so our prisoners claimed) if the rest of our regiment and the chasseurs could have got across the bridge and out of the village more quickly.

We camped that night at the spot where we had captured these troopers. They turned out to be from the Prussian Guard Cavalry, and included hussars, dragoons, and a few Berlin cossacks, whose beards were longer than those of the Don cossacks. Altogether they numbered 150.[6]

On 30 May we went with the Emperor's a.d.c., Flahaut, on a reconnaissance toward Jaworz, while Marshal Marmont approached the same town along a road to our right. A mile outside Lignica we saw some cossacks to our front. General Flahaut climbed to the top of a windmill, from which he could see several cossack regiments with masses of regular cavalry behind them. He said he had orders from the Emperor to contact Marmont, but that it would be impossible to break through all that cavalry with my two squadrons. I suggested he write a message [to Marmont] and give it to two of my more reliable German speaking troopers who would try to sneak past the Russians and reach Marmont during the night. The General agreed to my suggestion and I sent the Bialkowski brothers, who were from Czacza near Smigel. One of them was a n.c.o. They got through safely to Marmont and returned on the third day with his reply. By then we were only two miles from Wroclaw [Breslau], which Marshal Ney's advance guard had occupied. The Emperor stayed with the Guard in Neumark.

From Neumark I was ordered to escort the Equerry, Caulaincourt, to the castle of Leuthen, and later Pleswitz, where he was to negotiate a peace with General Shuvalov. General Shuvalov came with a couple of hundred cossacks, who also dismounted. We chattered with their officers, who told us where they were based in Poland. It emerged that they knew some houses that were familiar to me, and I asked a cossack colonel if he would be so kind as to deposit a letter from me to my father at the central Russian post office. I offered to leave the letter unsealed. He promised to do this, but urged me to seal the letter: he would write the address, and no one would open it. I entered the palace and asked the Emperor's secretary, Baron Fain, for some paper, and stayed to write my letter. While I was alone in the room with the secretary (Caulaincourt was next door with Shuvalov and Kleist), Baron Fain showed me the Emperor's proposed peace terms that had been submitted to Emperor Alexander. At the very beginning he offered Alexander the whole of the Duchy of Warsaw and was prepared either for Alexander to take the title, "King of Poland", or for the Duchy to be absorbed into his Empire.

The Imperial secretary, who regarded me as a Frenchman, having seem me for so many years in the service of the Emperor, could not imagine what a dreadful revelation it was to me to see this document. I went outside to hide my confusion, and I was so lost in thought that I only pulled myself together when the cossack colonel approached and asked for the letter. I gave it to him with a note telling him what address to write. This letter reached my father. The cossacks were always very polite to us, as if they remembered the days when they had been our allies.[7]

An armistice was signed, but no peace treaty as the Emperor had proposed. We marched back to Dresden. There I wrote my request to be discharged and submitted it to Marshal Soult.

6 The Leichtes Garde Kavallerie Regiment consisted from February 1813 of a squadron each of ulans, dragoons, hussars and 'cossacks'. In March 1815, the first three were expanded to form regiments, and the 'cossacks' were attached to the Ulans.

7 A rose-tinted supposition. The Cossacks could equally well remember the days when they had been reluctant vassals, and later implacable enemies of the Polish-Lithuanian Commonwealth. But Cossacks and Poles had the shared experience of living in close proximity to a mighty Russia, against whom both had fought even more often than they had each other.

OFFICER AND TROOPER OF THE POLISH LANCERS

He was very surprised and tried to persuade me to remain in service. I could not compromise secretary Fain and tell everybody about the proposed peace terms, as he had shown them to me in confidence. But I did decide to tell Captain Jordan, who was a close friend, as well as

General Chlopicki. Chlopicki was outraged and declared he would rather break rocks than serve that man any longer. Both Chlopicki and Jordan tendered their resignations.

When Marshal Soult approved my discharge papers, I went to Paris where I stayed at the house of the Caramans, the friends of my youth. Only then, after enduring too many punishing campaigns, did I succumb to sickness and was indisposed for several months. I'm sure very few of those who had lived through the Russian campaign escaped the fever, which could strike as much as twelve months later.

Peace was concluded in Paris. The Prussians were given Poznan, but the city was still occupied by Russians. I left Paris for Great Britain, intending to wait there until the Russians evacuated Poznan. I had been told that the Russian governor was forcing all Poles to swear an oath of allegiance, and I preferred to deny myself the ceremony.

I stayed in London throughout the winter of 1814 to 1815. I went to several sessions of their Parliament. They were just debating the Corn Laws, which were beneficial, and at that time even necessary, to the landowners. However, the occupants of the towns, especially the manufacturers, opposed them vigorously, and on many occasions arranged violent demonstrations by the inhabitants of the capital. They would gather in their thousands and smash the house windows of the members of parliament who supported the Laws. They also smashed windows at the Palace of Westminster. The whole city was in turmoil. On one occasion, wanting to watch these goings on close to, I had to take cover behind some steps and press myself against a locked door to stop myself being carried away by the crowd which filled the street, waving banners that proclaimed: "No to the Corm Laws! Down with the Government!" At their center was Bardett [sic], the populist M.P. who opposed the Corn Laws.

The 10th Hussars and the Lifeguards were camped on the streets and stationed squadrons at the main popular gathering places and the houses of M.P.s. A constable would always walk in front of each squadron with a white pennant, and wherever the people gathered together to create a disturbance or attack a minister's or MP's residence, this man would read the Riot Act. He read it once, then twice, but the people shouted so loudly that nobody could hear him. But the time he finished reading it for the third time, however, the streets would have cleared completely and the demonstrators disappeared. For they knew that after the third reading, the cavalry would charge straight at anybody who had not obeyed the instructions to disperse. In the evenings. people gathered outside the Houses of Parliament would barrack those MP's who supported the Law as they entered the building. Very often these MPs had to enter by the back doors. This freedom made a striking impression on me. Anyone who wasn't a MP was permitted to enter the House of Commons if he wished. I met a few MPs there, and sometimes ate with them at about seven in the evening while the House was in session. There was a restaurant for MPs in the same building. One day there was to be a debate on the Polish question. Apparently, Britain, France, and Austria wanted the Duchy of Warsaw to retain its independent status, and not allow it to be placed under Russian rule. So I received a formal invitation to attend the session on that occasion. In the Lower House there is a place set aside for strangers and foreigners, who are admitted at the personal invitation of the Speaker. In the event nothing of much interest was raised; all they discussed was the state of the negotiations in Vienna.

I was in Bath staying with Caraman's sister, Lady Sommery, when the news arrived that the Emperor had left Elba and landed at Frejus. Knowing the French army as I did, I did not

MARSHAL OUDINOT

doubt that they would nearly all rally to him. I had left my carriage, my possessions, and three Polish servants in Paris, so I returned to them quickly but left the city on the morning of 20 March. The Emperor entered Paris at 8 p.m. that day. I met some officers I knew who had been with the Emperor the previous day. They told me how all the troops he met on his way had gone over to him.

In Metz I learned that Marshal Oudinot had just returned from Nancy. I went to call on him, as he had always been kind to me. I found him bed-ridden. He described sadly how he had been made commander of the Old Guard by Louis XVIII and given Metz as his garrison town. He had received orders to march to Troyes to join Marshal Ney, who had urged Louis to give him command of the Army, promising faithfully to defeat Napoleon. On the march Oudinot heard that the Grenadiers were overjoyed to be marching to rejoin their Emperor. He therefore concluded that they would go over to the Emperor immediately, so ordered a countermarch and resolved to return to Metz. But the head of the column refused to obey his commands, and the Grenadiers surrounded him, urging him to lead them to the Emperor. He reminded them of their oath of loyalty to Louis XVIII, but his words went unheeded. When the Grenadiers realized he would not go with them, they continued on their way and he returned sadly to Metz. As he passed down the column, the solders surrounded him and begged him to go with them, but he refused, saying he did not know how to break his word. The Emperor had released him from his allegiance and now he must remain loyal to the King of France. When he had left the column of the Guard he encountered the 1st Regiment of Hussars, whose colonel was his son. He ordered him to gather his officers, explained the situation to them, and declared that an oath was sacred to a man of honor. The officers, among whom were many from the old nobility of France, listened to his advice and persuaded the soldiers to obey their colonel's order and turn back to Metz. Shortly after, he encountered the 2nd Regiment of Hussars, who could not be persuaded to turn around. Indeed their officers called on their colleagues in the 1st to join them and march to meet the Emperor. They came to blows, and a dozen or so officers on both sides were wounded. In the end, the 2nd Regiment marched off after the Guard and the 1st returned with the Marshal to Metz.

I recount this incident to try to help explain the subsequent defeat at Waterloo. An army in which loyalties are divided is weak, however courageous. Apparently at Waterloo, a whole brigade of dragoons under General Bourmont, as well as several artillery batteries, ran away at the very start of the day. It is strange to note that it was the artillery, the Emperor's favorite arm, that was the most opposed to him in that campaign.[8] There is no honor in deserting a post in the heat of battle. My friend Caraman performed far better. Back in 1814, just before the abdication when the Emperor at Fontainebleau had been deserted by the men who owed him everything, Caraman was still reporting for duty. The Emperor was surprised by this because the Caraman family had always been royalists. He asked, "Why have you not flown to join your new master?"

"Because Your Majesty has not released me. I wanted to prove to you that we are the equals of those you created." This reply pleased the Emperor and he gave Caraman a personal recommendation to give to Louis XVIII. When Napoleon returned from Elba, Caraman commanded the artillery of the Royal Garde du Corps and followed the King into exile in Ghent. Louis sent the artillery back into France at the frontier, but Caraman went with him to Ghent and returned to Paris with him. All in all, the Emperor had survived only a hundred days between landing from Elba and embarking for Saint Helena.

I stopped off in Berlin during my journey home, but saw nobody I knew. When the Russians vacated Poznan, I returned home.

The End

8 A striking claim, not borne out by any of the numerous first hand accounts of Waterloo, but interesting nonetheless as a third hand contemporary explanation for Napoleon's defeat. Bourmont defected alone, without taking any dragoons with him. The artillery was prevented from operating effectively on the morning of 18 June 1815 by mud, and the battle started late to allow time for the ground to dry. The failure of the guns to begin firing at daybreak could well have been blamed on the treachery of gunners rather than on the weather. Chlapowski would have heard accounts of the defeat at a time when all France was talking of betrayal. The earlier description of Oudinot's dilemma fits what we know of the marshal's refusal to change sides again in 1815, but old age and exhaustion probably played as great a part as honor in his decision.

CHLAPOWSKI IN 1831

CHLAPOWSKI IN BATTLE DURING THE 1830 INSURRECTION

Chlapowski's Service Record

Adam Desire Chlapowski was born March 31, 1790[1] in Turwa [Turwii], Department of Posen, in the Commonwealth of Poland.

Poland having been partitioned, he was enrolled in June 1802 as a cadet in the Briesewitz Dragoon Regiment in the service of Prussia. At this time he was seconded to the Institute of Officers of the Berlin Inspectorate.

In November 1806, he returned to Posen to serve in the Posen Garde d'Honneur. This was a unit of about 100 horsemen which replaced Napoleon's French Guard as he progressed through Poland after his victories over the Prussians.

Serving as Lieutenant in the 9th Polish Infantry Regiment of the new Duchy of Warsaw, he commanded a company of voltigeurs. He was taken prisoner at the siege of Gdansk [Danzig] and was liberated by the treaty of Tilsit.

In December 1807, he was promoted captain and nominated by prince Poniatowski to be aide de camp to General Dabrowski [who was apparently Chlapowski's brother-in-law].

On February 1808, he was selected to serve as one of Napoleon's orderly officers in the Spanish campaign.

He was awarded the French Legion of Honor on March 3, 1807, the Polish Virtuti Militari on April 3, 1809, and made a Baron of the French Empire August 15, 1810.

Appointed squadron commander [chef d'escadron] of the 1st Regiment of Polish Light Horse Lancers of the Imperial Guard on January 13, 1811, he served with this regiment in the Russian campaign of 1812 and the 1813 campaign where he distinguished himself at the battle of Reichenbach.

Disillusioned with Napoleon's abandonment of Poland's independence, he asked to be released from Napoleon's service in July of 1813.

He served as Colonel of Lancers, General of Brigade, and General of Division during the 1830 Polish Insurrection against the Russians.

Chlapowski died in 1879.

---

1   Several dates are given for Chlapowski's birth. This is the date in the French records.

Compiled by Matt Sobieszczyk, with assistance from Jan Lorys, from A. Rembowski, Sources... du Regiment des Chevau-legers, Warsaw, 1899; Chelminski & Malibran, L'Armee du Duche de Varsovie, Paris, 1913; S. Kirkor, Polscy Donatariusze Napoleona, London, 1974.

THE CHLAPOWSKI FAMILY IN AMERICA

In 1877, Karol Bozenta Chlapowski settled in Southern California, where he became part of a small Polish colony in Anaheim. His friends there included the novelist and Nobel laureate, Henryk Sienkiewicz. Karol's wife, Helena Modjeska became America's foremost Shakespearean actress, despite her Polish accent. They had no descendents, but their house still stands in its oak grove on the banks on the banks of Santiago Creek in the foothills of the Santa Ana mountains. The house is being renovated by its owner, Orange County, in preparation for its opening to the public, and a non-profit group, the Helena Modjeska Foundation, has been founded to assist in the preservation of the house and its traditions.

THE HELENA MODJESKA FOUNDATION
P.O.Box 9582
NEWPORT BEACH, CALIFORNIA 92658

Karol Chlapowski referred to General Dezydery Chlapowski as his uncle, though the relationship in fact might have been cousins several times removed, both being great-great grandsons of Kazimierz Chlapowski, who died in 1701. Karol's sister, Anna, married her distant cousin, Kazimierz, who was the son of Dezydery Chlapowski, in 1862. Their family settled in Krakow.

GIBERNE [CARTRIDGE POUCH] OF AN OFFICER OF THE POLISH LANCERS

PANOPLY OF A POLISH LANCER
CZAPSKA, OFFICER'S SWORD, AND LEGION D'HONNEUR

POLISH LANCERS FIGHTING AUSTRIANS